Finding & Responding to God's Presence & Love

Robert J. Sullivan

TRILOGY CHRISTIAN PUBLISHERS
Tustin, CA

Trilogy Christian Publishers
A Wholly Owned Subsidiary of Trinity Broadcasting Network
2442 Michelle Drive
Tustin, CA 92780

Finding & Responding to God's Presence & Love

Copyright © 2024 by Robert Sullivan

All scripture quotations are taken from the New Revised Standard Version Updated Edition. Copyright © 2021 National Council of Churches of Christ in the United States of America. Used by permission. All rights reserved worldwide.

All rights reserved, including the right to reproduce this book or portions thereof in any form whatsoever.

For information, address Trilogy Christian Publishing

Rights Department, 2442 Michelle Drive, Tustin, CA 92780.

Trilogy Christian Publishing/ TBN and colophon are trademarks of Trinity Broadcasting Network.

For information about special discounts for bulk purchases, please contact Trilogy Christian Publishing.

Trilogy Disclaimer: The views and content expressed in this book are those of the author and may not necessarily reflect the views and doctrine of Trilogy Christian Publishing or the Trinity Broadcasting Network.

10 9 8 7 6 5 4 3 2 1

Library of Congress Cataloging-in-Publication Data is available.

ISBN 979-8-89333-507-1

ISBN (ebook) 979-8-89333-508-8

Contents

Prologue vii

Finding Theological First Principles xiii

    The Reason for Establishing First Principles xiii

    Five Subjective First Principles xiv

    Three Objective First Principles xiv

Introduction xvi

**Part One:
Finding God's Presence and Love
through God's Evolving Creation**

Chapter One. Finding God's Presence and Love in Seven Biblical Creation/Re-Creation Narratives 3

    The First Genesis Creation Narrative 6

    The Second Genesis Creation Narrative 8

    The Third Genesis Creation Narrative 11

    The Fourth Re-Creation Narrative 14

    The Fifth Creation Narrative 20

    The Sixth Re-Creation Narrative 24

    The Seventh Re-Creation Narrative 26

Chapter Two. Finding God's Presence and Love in God's Theocentric Creation 33

Part Two:
Finding God's Presence and Love through Theological Conditions

Chapter Three. The Human Theological Conditions Necessary to Accept God's Offer of Grace 43

Chapter Four. The Theological Intersection Between Humanity and Divinity 60

Chapter Five. The Divine Theological Conditions that Make God's Offer of Grace Available to Humanity 70

God's Love Is Present throughout God's Creation 71

God's Love Is Present through God's Holy Spirit 78

God's Love Is Present through the Ministry of the Historical Jesus of Nazareth 84

Part Three:
Finding God's Presence and Love through God's Religious Tradition

Chapter Six. Finding God's Presence and Love in Catholic Sacraments 115

Chapter Seven. Finding God's Presence and Love in Catholic Tradition 123

Finding God's Presence and Love in the Documents of Catholic Ecumenical Councils 125

Finding God's Presence and Love in Papal Encyclicals .. 129

Finding God's Presence and Love in the Documents of Catholic Mystics 133

Part Four:
Responding to God's Presence and Love as Individuals

Chapter Eight. Developing a Foundational Individual Relationship with God 152

    Responding to God's Presence and Love through Our Faith 153

    Responding to God's Presence and Love through Our Trust 158

    Responding to God's Presence and Love through Our Hope 162

    Responding to God's Presence and Love through Our Love 166

Chapter Nine. Developing a Deeper Individual Relationship with God 170

    Responding to God's Presence and Love through Our Prayers 171

    Responding to God's Presence and Love through Our Obedience 176

    Responding to God's Presence and Love through Our Discipleship 179

    Responding to God's Presence and Love through Reading and Studying the Word of God 182

    Responding to God's Presence and Love through Becoming a Self-for-Others 195

Responding to God's Presence and Love through
Our Joy and Thanksgiving..198

Part Five:
Responding to God's Presence
and Love in Community

Chapter Ten. We Need to Respond to God's Presence
and Love in Community 203

Bibliography..206

Prologue

God's presence and love is always available, but we have to search for it. Why do we search for God? We search for God because we were created and designed to search for meaning and purpose in our lives (e.g., through our restlessness). We were also created to enjoy a loving and eternal home, which is sometimes referred to as heaven in the book of Wisdom 2:23a (NRSV)[1] "²³for <u>God created us for incorruption</u>, and <u>made us in the image of his own eternity</u>." So, we necessarily search for a loving God full of kindness, mercy, and forgiveness. In this book, I describe several ways to search for God's presence and love in our daily lives, and I describe several ways to respond to God's presence and love once we have found Him, even though He was never really missing.

No one chooses to be born, and someone must care for us until we can care for ourselves, or until we are forced to care for ourselves. Throughout our lives, we learn that we cannot escape from our relentless ques-

---

[1] I reference the New Revised Standard Version (NRSV) in all my scriptural quotations.

tions. The purpose of my book is to help people find answers to some of their questions (e.g., why don't I feel God's presence and love in my life?) My answer is, we can always find God's presence and love in our lives, and we can learn how to know and love God, which will help us to know and love ourselves and others. In my opinion, we will never satisfactorily answer any of our questions until we find access to the hidden treasures in God's presence and love, which lead us toward God's original incorruptible eternal design for humanity in Genesis 1:26-27 and Wisdom 2:23a.

We spend our lives searching for the best answers that we can find to our questions, or we do our best to ignore our questions. God has the answers that we are searching for in Jeremiah 29:13-14a "[13]When you search for me; you will find me; if you seek me with all your heart. [14a]<u>I will let you find me, says the LORD</u>." When we do find God's presence and love in our everyday lives, we need to hold onto Him in Proverbs 3:5-7; Psalm 32:8; and Romans 8:37-39, because people will try to separate us from God. Thousands of years ago, a psalmist faced difficulties in his life and he described his situation in Psalm 42:3 [3]"My tears have been my food day and night, while people say to me continually, <u>'Where is your God?'</u>" The most important question in our search for God is whether we are open to the unconditional offer of God's presence and love in our life.

We live in an ever-changing imperfect world. William Shakespeare summarized the imperfections in our lives in Hamlet's soliloquy: "the heart-ache and the thousand natural shocks that flesh is heir to." (*Hamlet*, Act III, Scene 1.) If we begin to plumb the depths of Shakespeare's exquisite summary on life's daily challenges, we can begin to categorize "the heart-ache and the thousand natural shocks that flesh is heir to" including: <u>our emotions</u> (e.g., loneliness, insecurity, disappointments, fear, guilt, rejection, sorrow, trials, burdens, despair, and the suffering caused by what people do to each other); <u>our temptations</u> (e.g., power, greed, lust, jealousy, envy); <u>the never-ending dichotomies in our lives</u> (e.g., good and evil, male and female); <u>the never-ending incongruities in our lives</u> (e.g., chaos from natural disasters, chaos from devastating wars, chaos from man-made atrocities, and the indescribable pain of parents outliving their children); <u>the evil in the world</u> (e.g., authoritarian political systems, totalitarian political systems); and the fear of <u>death</u> (nobody gets out alive.) These ongoing imperfections may cause us to hold God in disrepute, but we must avoid the quicksand of despair and hopelessness and learn to trust that God's presence and love remain firmly rooted in our everyday lives. We need to minimize our focus on life's imperfections and focus on our blessings and God's eternal promises to us (e.g.,

Hebrews 13:5 "I will never leave you or forsake you.") Today, artists continue to describe the imperfections that actualize our human emotions (e.g., loneliness) in their poetry, in their art, and in their song lyrics (e.g., in the lyrics and imagery of the Hank Williams' song, "I'm so lonesome I could cry.") The prophet Isaiah described God's explanation for the ongoing imperfections in our daily lives in Isaiah 55:8 "[8]For my thoughts are not your thoughts, nor are your ways my ways, says the LORD." In other words, the ongoing imperfections in our lives are a mystery, but they are not necessarily flaws in God's creation.

We need to ask ourselves the question: What is the center of the universe? The answers to this question have changed over time with better scientific information and the answer to this question influences our worldview. Ptolemy [100-168 CE], advanced a <u>geocentric view</u> of the universe: the sun revolves around the earth; so, the earth became the center of the universe. Copernicus [1473-1543], having more scientific information, advanced a <u>heliocentric view</u> of the universe: the earth revolves around the sun; so, the sun became the center of the universe. Rene Descartes [1596–1650] advanced a view based on his axiom "I think therefore I am and I can't be certain of anything else"; so, each person became the center of the universe to themselves. However, for Judeo-Christian believers, God is the center of the universe; so, the universe revolves around God's presence and love.

We need to ask ourselves the question: If we cannot find God's presence and love here and now, then how can we hope to find His presence and love in eternity? We will recognize God's presence and love in our lives when we accept the idea that our lives are being lived out in a world created and designed by God for God. Isaiah tells us to seek the Lord while we can in Isaiah 55:6, which is right now. The psalmist prayed to God for guidance in Psalm 25:4 "<u>Make me to know your ways</u>, O LORD; teach me your paths." Roger Haight SJ, reminds us that we do not turn to Jesus for information; we turn to Jesus, because an encounter with Jesus is an encounter with God's presence and love. A simple way to understand humanity is to observe children, because children are not born with hate in their hearts. Children learn how to hate from their environment, or worse, they are taught how to hate. In Romans 1:18-25, St. Paul was certain that people consciously exchange their knowledge of God for a counterfeit god and God will eventually give them up to their lives of degradation.

Throughout my book, I reference the Word of God, because the Word of God is the underlying source of my strength and joy. I want to thank all the people, who helped me understand God's presence and love in my life; especially my parents, my teachers at Boston

College, School of Theology and Ministry (e.g., Dan Harrington SJ, Roger Haight SJ, Dick Clifford SJ, John O'Donnell SJ, Chris Matthews), my students, and my friends, especially Eileen Guerin, who edited an early version of my book. The mistakes are mine alone. My continuing thanks to my wife, who always encourages me. And my very special thanks to my Jewish stepfather, Dr. Moshe Ben Mordecai, Halevi, who escaped NAZI Germany in 1938 and explained Judaism to me in a practical way. For example, he often reminded me of the things that no Jewish boy would ever say.

Finding Theological First Principles

The Reason for Establishing First Principles

Most everyone has core beliefs (e.g., I believe or I don't believe there is higher power in the universe.) We don't necessarily think about or articulate our core beliefs, but they certainly influence our thinking and our approach to life's challenges. Before thinking about and studying theology, that is, studying the nature of God, I believe it is necessary to begin with first principles (e.g., we need to establish and refine a worldview that helps us search for God's presence and love in our daily lives.) I am not suggesting that we begin with a refined set of first principles; rather, we develop and refine our first principles as we learn more about the nature of God. We can think about first principles as boundaries that guide our search for God's presence and love in our lives. In my opinion, if we do not develop our own first principles, then we're very likely using somebody else's first principles. In this part of my book, I identify my own first principles, which may appear arbitrary and certainly others could work, but these eight first principles have helped me to understand God's presence and love in my own life subjectively and objectively.

Five Subjective First Principles

There are at least five first principles that help me to understand God subjectively: <u>First</u>, we're created ex nihilo [out of nothing] in Genesis 1:26-27, in the image of God in 2 Corinthians 4:4; 1 Corinthians 15:49; and Colossians 1:15-16, and in the likeness of God in Ephesians 4:24, therefore, we're radically dependent on God for our existence, our fulfillment, and our salvation; <u>Second</u>, we know and experience God in our innermost being long before anyone teaches us about God [the Father] in Romans 1:18-25; <u>Third</u>, God's presence and love is always available to us; <u>Fourth</u>, Jesus Christ is my positive, loving, personal Lord and Savior; and <u>Fifth</u>, the easiest way to search for and understand God's presence and love in our daily lives is to continue our search to understand ourselves (e.g., through our <u>restlessness</u> (e.g., our questions, our disappointments) and through our <u>abstractions)</u>, because our restlessness and our abstractions are intended to lead us to an encounter with God's presence and love.

Three Objective First Principles

There are at least three first principles that help me to understand God objectively: <u>First</u>, any knowledge of

God is not objective, because God is not an object as set forth in John 4:24 "²⁴<u>God is spirit</u>, and those who worship God must worship God in spirit and truth"; <u>Second</u>, we cannot explain the mystery of God nor can we explain the mystery of God away; and <u>Third</u>, doctrines about God are culturally conditioned; so, they represent the best knowledge that people living in different parts of the world had at different points in time.

Introduction

My book is not an exhaustive theological treatise, because I lack the capacity to plumb the depths of the Absolute Mystery of God (e.g., St. Thomas Aquinas tells us that God's essence and existence are the same.)[2] In my opinion, this is an interesting assertion, which cannot be proven or disproven by me. Instead, this book is an overview of "where to" or "how to" find some of the answers to our relentless never-ending questions (e.g., where did I come from, why am I here, where am I going?) So, the purpose of my book is to assure everyone that they can always find God's presence and love in their lives, and hopefully my book provides helpful ways to search for God's presence and love. Throughout the ten chapters of my book, I identify specific ways to find God's presence and love in our lives and specific ways to respond to God's presence and love in our lives once we have found God in our lives.

<u>In part one of my book</u>, chapter one describes a seven-step evolving biblical <u>creation/re-creation</u>

---

[2] St. Thomas Aquinas, *De Ente et Essentia* (On Being and Essence)

process. However, I am not limiting the evolving biblical creation process to seven scriptural narratives; rather, I am limiting my focus to seven specific evolving creation/re-creation narratives in the scriptures. My intent is to illustrate the evolution of God's relationship with humanity during each step of God's creation/re-creation process (e.g., in the first creation narrative God gave humanity dominion over His creation, in Genesis 1:26, 28.) Chapter two asks the question whether humanity was given dominion over an anthropocentric creation or a theocentric creation?

In part two of my book, I examine the intersection between humanity and divinity. Chapter three examines the human side of the intersection between humanity and divinity by examining foundational theological conditions that make humans different from other beings (e.g., our human freedom) and additional theological conditions that make humans different from other beings (e.g., God's gifts to us.) Chapter four examines God's offer of grace to us at the actual intersection of humanity and divinity. Grace is the amazing underlying wiring that connects humanity to divinity in our everyday experience. In addition, I briefly examine the two-thousand-year history of the evolving Christian theology of grace focusing on how grace impacts humanity from six different perspectives (e.g., St. Augustine, Karl Rahner SJ.) Chapter five examines the divine side of the intersection between humanity and divinity (e.g., God's presence and love for us through God the Father, through God's Holy Spirit, and through the historical Jesus.)

<u>In part three of my book</u>, I remind everyone that they can find God's presence and love through the religious practices, liturgies, and traditions of any religious community of faith. However, I am a practicing Catholic; so, chapter six describes how to find and worship God through the seven sacraments of the Catholic Church. Chapter seven describes how to find and worship God through Catholic tradition (e.g., through the documents of two of the twenty-one Ecumenical Councils, through the documents of countless Papal Encyclicals, and through the documents that describe the revelations of some of the mystics found in the early Catholic Church, the sixteenth century Catholic Church, and the modern-day Catholic Church.)

<u>In part four of my book</u>, I describe at least ten ways to <u>individually</u> respond to God's presence and love in our everyday lives, because responding to God's offer of grace in our lives leads us home. In chapter eight, I describe four ways to individually respond to God's presence and love in our lives in order to develop a foundational, positive, loving, personal relationship with God: <u>First</u>, through our faith, <u>Second</u>, through our trust, <u>Third</u>, through our hope, and <u>Fourth</u>, through our

love. In chapter nine, I describe six additional ways to <u>individually</u> respond to God's offer of grace that build on our foundation of faith, trust, hope, and love: <u>First</u>, through our prayers, <u>Second</u>, through our obedience, <u>Third</u>, through our discipleship, <u>Fourth</u>, through reading and studying the Word of God (e.g., Isaiah 55:10-11), <u>Fifth</u>, through becoming a self-for-others, and <u>Sixth</u>, through our joy and thanksgiving.

<u>In part five of my book</u>, chapter ten describes our need to go beyond our individual responses to God's presence and love and worship God in a faith community, because we live our lives in community. And, the most obvious place to find God's presence and love is in God's metaphorical home, the church, the synagogue, etc. We pray and worship God in community through the beautiful liturgies, music, and traditions in our respective churches and synagogues. All places of worship dedicated to the one true God help us to understand God's ongoing love story with humanity.

Part One:

Finding God's Presence and Love through God's Evolving Creation

CHAPTER ONE

Finding God's Presence and Love in Seven Biblical Creation/Re-Creation Narratives

Introduction

We begin our search to find God's presence and love in our lives by establishing a worldview about the creation of the universe and humanity! Do we live in a universe created and designed by God or do we live in a universe that <u>somehow</u> came into being? <u>Religious people believe</u> that God created the universe and humanity. <u>Non-religious people believe</u> that <u>somehow</u> the universe and humanity came into being (e.g., materialism, scientific atheism, spontaneous creation, some variation of Plato's demiurge.) We have no conclusive scientific evidence to support any worldview on how the universe and humanity were created; therefore, no worldview can be conclusively proven or disproven. Judeo-Christian believers <u>necessarily</u> come to their view of creation through their faith and trust in a God of Absolute Mystery. Non-religious believers <u>necessarily</u> come to their view of the creation through their faith and trust in something, which is often disguised with scientific extrapolations and projections, but not with settled science (e.g., Dr. Stephen C. Meyer's books refute the claims of Darwinism, Neo-Darwinism, and post Neo-Darwinism, etc.)[3] Of course, the idea that God created the world and humanity is supported throughout the scriptures (e.g., Psalm 24:1-2 "¹The earth is the Lord's and all that is in it, the world, and those who live in it; ²for he has founded it on the seas, and established it on the rivers.")

We are left with our relentless questions, because we do not have definitive answers to how the universe and humanity occurred. An excellent starting point to search for answers to our questions can be found in Psalm 14:2 "²The LORD looks down from heaven on humankind to see if there are any who are wise, who seek after God." In other words, God is searching for us, if we are searching for God. In part one of my book, I explain my understanding of the beginning and the end of God's theological creation/re-creation process from

---

3 Dr. Stephen C, Meyer, "Signature in the Cell," "Darwin's Doubt," "Return of the God Hypotheses"

the point of view of seven selected biblical creation/re-creation scriptural narratives. My focus is to try and understand the evolving nature of God's relationship with humanity throughout God's creation/re-creation process (e.g., God describes the beginning of His creation of the universe and humanity as very good in Gen. 1:31 "[31]God saw everything that he had made, and indeed, it was very good.") However, we know that evil and chaos exist in our world; so, our search for God's presence and love cannot ignore Shakespear's summary of the human condition: "the heart-ache and the thousand natural shocks that flesh is heir to." (*Hamlet*, Act III, Scene 1, William Shakespeare)

In theology, this is called the theodicy problem [why does evil exist in God's creation?] We must find the strength to search for God's presence and love no matter how much we're distracted or discouraged by the unwanted events that creep into our daily lives.

My search for God's evolving presence and love begins by examining seven selected biblical creation/re-creation narratives in God's evolving biblical creation process: First, the first Genesis creation narrative in Genesis 1:1–2:4a; Second, the second Genesis creation narrative in Genesis 2:4b–11:32; Third, the creation of the people of God in Genesis 12-50 and the Exodus narrative, which describes the creation of the nation of Israel in Exodus 1–40; Leviticus 1–27; Numbers 1–36;

Fourth, the re-creation of a faithful, repentant, remnant of the people of God, who returned to Israel after seventy years of exile in Babylon in Second Isaiah 40–55; Fifth, the creation narrative in the prologue of John's Gospel in John 1:1-5, 14; Sixth, the re-creation narrative in John 3:1-21, when Jesus taught Nicodemus and us that we need to be re-created from above [spiritually], because God is Spirit in John 4:24; and Seventh, the final re-creation narrative describes our individual re-creation [resurrection] into eternal life in the kingdom [reign] of God in 1 Corinthians 15 and John 11:25-27; 18:36.

The First Genesis Creation Narrative

The first two Genesis narratives have multiple sources but describing them is beyond the scope of my book. I'm focusing on the narratives as they are presented in the NRSV, which describe how God's creation process began to evolve.

In the first Genesis creation narrative, God's presence and love can be understood as God creating a habitable world out of an inhabitable world by systematically removing darkness and chaos from an inhabitable world through a series of steps: First, God created light and separated light from darkness; Second, God separated the waters in order to create the sky and the land; Third, God created plants and trees of every kind, which contained seeds that bore fruit and vegetables; <u>Fourth</u>, God created the sun to rule the day and the moon and the stars to rule the night; <u>Fifth</u>, God created every living creature that moves in the land, in the waters, and in the air; <u>Sixth</u>, God created humanity in the image of God in 2 Corinthians 4:4; 1 Corinthians 15:49; and Colossians 1:15 and in the likeness of God in Ephesians 4:24. When the first creation process was completed, God gave humanity dominion over the fish of the sea, the birds of the air, the cattle, all the wild animals of the earth, and all the creeping things that creep on the earth in Genesis 1:28 and Psalm 8:6-9.

God created humanity to enjoy a loving and eternal home in Wisdom 2:23a "²³for <u>God created us for incorruption</u>, and <u>made us in the image of his own eternity</u>." By contrast, we can study a Sumerian [ancient Mesopotamia] creation myth, called "The Eridu Genesis," which is dated around 1600 BCE. Humanity was created by the gods but humanity became too noisy; so, some of the gods wanted to destroy humanity with a flood. In my opinion, humanity was created to become slaves of the ruling gods. However, in the first Genesis narrative (cf. Genesis 1:1-2:3), God created the universe, including humanity, to live freely, joyfully, eternally, and fruitfully by multiplying and filling the earth and living in a loving monotheistic relationship with God.

<u>In the first Genesis narrative, God's presence and love is the foundation of God's creation of the universe and humanity and God assured us that His creation</u>

was good in Genesis 1:31. God blessed humanity and made us limited co-creators with Him by propagating humanity and filling the earth and having dominion over the fish, the birds, the cattle, the wild animals, and all creeping things on the earth. There is no mention of humanity being kicked out of Paradise. However, there's no explicit description of God's presence and love for humanity in a relationship beyond Creator and creature. Nevertheless, humanity needs to be in a positive, loving, faithful, personal relationship with God, because we are created, fulfilled, and sustained by God.

The Second Genesis Creation Narrative

In the second Genesis creation narrative, God's presence and love is described in a much larger literary unit in Genesis 2:4b–11:32. In Genesis 2:4-6, God created the heavens and the earth. In Genesis 2:7, God formed man from the dust of the earth by breathing into his nostrils the breath of life. Then God planted a garden [Paradise], which grew every tree that is pleasant to the sight and good for food, and there He put the man in Genesis 2:8 to till and keep the garden. God created all the animals on the earth, the birds in the air, and God created woman to help the man in Genesis 2:21-22.

In the second Genesis creation narrative, God gave the man a single commandment not to eat from the tree of knowledge of good and evil in Genesis 2:15-17. However, humanity disobeyed God's single commandment in an attempt to become equal to God. God punished humanity for their disobedience by kicking them out of Paradise in Genesis 3:1-24 and by adding burdens and death to our lives in Genesis 3:19 "¹⁹By the sweat of your face you shall eat bread until you return to the ground, for out of it you were taken; <u>you are dust, and to dust you shall return</u>." Sin and evil were always present in God's creation, but they weren't actualized until Adam and Eve disobeyed God. Once sin was actualized, death and burdens came to humanity. It remains a mystery why sin and evil were designed into God's creation.

Humanity did not do well outside of Paradise from the very beginning (e.g., Cain murdered his brother Abel in Genesis 4:1-16.) The sons of God [angels] had offspring with human women in Genesis 6:1-4. Eventually, humanity became so evil outside of Paradise that God intervened to destroy His creation in Genesis 6:5-7 "⁵The LORD saw that the wickedness of humankind was great and that every inclination of the thoughts of their hearts was only evil continually. ⁶And the LORD was sorry that he had made humankind on the earth, and it grieved him to his heart. ⁷So the LORD said, 'I will blot out from the earth the human beings I have created—people together with animals and creeping things and birds of the air, for I am sorry that I have made them.'" But God found one righteous man, named Noah, and God decided to save Noah and his family and give humanity a second chance in Genesis 6:8-10. Noah and his family would bring humanity back to their original design to love God faithfully and obediently in Genesis 1:26-28 and Wisdom 2:23a. Unfortunately, humanity's second chance ended in a futile attempt to build a tower to the Absolute Mystery of God in Genesis 11:1-9, which was another futile attempt to become equal to God. Humanity's disobedience outside Paradise was arguably inevitable, because there is no recorded guidance from God on how humanity should behave righteously outside of Paradise. Specifically, there were no rules or commandments to help humanity find a better righteousness in their everyday lives outside of Paradise.

In the second Genesis creation narrative, God's presence and love for humanity evolved, because in addition to being limited co-creators with God by propagating the human race, humanity became limited co-creators with God by explicitly tilling and keeping the grounds of Paradise. In the second creation narrative, we can understand that humanity's experience outside of Paradise lacked explicit guidance and without God's explicit guidance, we're drawn to immoral and destructive action but we're also drawn to God's presence and love. However, since humanity is no longer in Paradise, we need God's help to be restored to eternal life with our Creator, because we are not capable of saving ourselves (e.g., Psalm 80:3 "Restore us, O God; let your face shine, that we may be saved.")

The Third Genesis Creation Narrative

In the third creation narrative, we find God's presence and love evolving into a very different relationship with humanity, because God intervened again to give humanity a third chance to obey and worship Him and live according to our original design in Genesis 1:26-28 and Wisdom 2:23a. This time God did not seek to destroy humanity. Instead, God found another righteous man named Abram and his wife named Sarai and from them He created the people of God, a chosen people. This newly created people of God were intended to become a light to the nations and a witness to the glory of Almighty God in a pagan world. However, God's chosen people still lacked God's specific guidance (e.g., rules or commandments) on how to be faithful, obedient, and righteous in a pagan world.

The third creation narrative begins with Abram obeying God and moving his family to an unknown place [Canaan] in Genesis 12:1 "¹Now the LORD said to Abram, "Go from your country and your kindred and your father's house to the land that I will show you."" In return for obeying God, Abram received seven unconditional promises from God in Genesis 12:2-3, 7 [first] ²I will make of you a great nation, and [second] I will bless you, [third] and make your name great [we're still talking about him], so that you will be a blessing. [fourth] ³I will bless those who bless you, [fifth] and the one who curses you I will curse; [sixth] "and in you all the families of the earth shall be blessed... [and seventh] ⁷Then the LORD appeared to Abram, and said, "To your offspring I will give this land." So he [Abraham] built there an altar to the LORD, who had appeared to him."

God's chosen people traveled from Canaan to Egypt in order to survive a famine. They remained in Egypt, but unfortunately God's chosen people became enslaved by the Pharaoh of Egypt for four hundred years, as we see in Genesis 15:13 and Acts 7:6.[4] Nevertheless, the people of God increased in numbers during their slavery in Egypt. Eventually, Pharaoh became concerned that the Israelites might turn against him if Egypt became engaged in an external war. Pharaoh's solution was to eliminate the people of God by killing all the male infants, in Exodus 1:15-22. Pharaoh's attack on the Israelites required God's intervention; so, God sent Moses to save His chosen people.

Moses led the people of God out of Egypt, but Joshua led the people of God into the Promised Land, Canaan, [ca. 1200 BCE], which was renamed Israel. Throughout

---

4 The number of years that Israel was in slavery is 430 years in Exodus 12:40 and Galatians 3:17.

the biblical exodus narrative (cf. Exodus, Leviticus, Numbers) and the book of Deuteronomy, God gave His chosen people six hundred and thirteen rules or commandments to guide them in their new lives in the Promised Land. In addition, the people of God also experienced His presence and love in a new way, that is, through God's covenantal relationship with His chosen people in Exodus 31:18 and in several covenant renewals including: Exodus 34:10-28; Deuteronomy 29:2-29, and Joshua. 8:30-35; 24:1-28. Throughout Deuteronomist history including Deuteronomy, Joshua, Judges, 1 & 2 Samuel, and 1 & 2 Kings, God continuously intervened to help His chosen people in the Promised Land, because they continuously fell into a cycle of disobedience, punishment, and redemption (e.g., throughout the book of Judges.)

Unfortunately, over time a schism caused the nation of Israel to become divided into two kingdoms. Eventually, the divided kingdoms could not sustain living in the Promised Land. The Israelites in the Northern Kingdom of Israel became so corrupt and disobedient to God that it was defeated, exiled, and assimilated into the Assyrian Empire [modern day Northern Iraq] [ca. 721 BCE.] At that time, the Israelites in the Southern Kingdom of Judah became a vassal state of Assyria. Sometime later, the Southern Kingdom of Judah also became corrupt and disobedient to God and it was defeated by Babylon [modern day Southern

Iraq.] In the process, the first temple was destroyed and many Israelites were exiled to Babylon, which became the first Diaspora [ca. 597/587 BCE.]

In the third creation narrative, God's presence and love for humanity became far more visible, and the relationship between God and humanity evolved in several ways. God created a chosen people to become a light to the nations and a witness to the glory of God in a pagan world. The chosen people were given the aforementioned six hundred and thirteen rules or commandments and they lived in a covenant relationship with God, Who continually came to Israel's aid in the Promised Land, because the Israelites continually fell into a cycle of disobedience, punishment, and redemption. The people of God experienced some success in the Promised Land in being a light to the nations and a witness to the glory of God (e.g., through their commandments, through their prayers (e.g., the psalms) and through some of their kings (e.g., King David in 1 Samuel 13:14 "the LORD has sought out a man after his own heart."))

The Fourth Re-Creation Narrative

In the fourth re-creation narrative [ca. 597/587 BCE], the Israelites remaining in the Southern Kingdom of Judah after their defeat from the Babylon Empire suffered greatly, because the first temple was destroyed,

Jerusalem was partially destroyed, and the Israelites lived in horrible conditions under Babylonian rule. This is recorded in the book of Lamentations. The Israelites exiled to Babylon also suffered greatly until their return to Israel in 539 BCE, when their punishment was complete. At some point in Israel's history the Southern Kingdom of Judah was renamed Israel. During this historical period, God's presence and love took on the form of judgment and punishment, because of Israel's disobedience and idolatry. This was prophesied in Isaiah 5, Isaiah's love song about God's metaphorical vineyard [Israel.]

My intent in this re-creation narrative is to briefly describe <u>First</u>, God's judgement on the Southern Kingdom of Judah and the Northern Kingdom of Israel; <u>Second</u>, the need for new leadership in Israel outside the succession of kings; <u>Third</u>, <u>the re-creation of the people of God</u>; <u>Fourth</u>, the necessary political changes to accomplish a new exodus from Babylon to Israel; <u>Fifth</u>, the necessary theological changes to accomplish the re-creation of the people of God; and <u>Sixth</u>, the return of a re-created, faithful, repentant, obedient, remnant of the people of God to Israel.

<u>First, God's judgment on the Southern Kingdom of Judah and the Northern Kingdom of Israel</u> is described in Isaiah 5 in the song of the vineyard. In Isaiah 6, Isaiah is somehow transported to heaven, where he received a commission from God to tell the Israelites what

their future would be if they remained disobedient to God. Isaiah 27:2-6 legitimized God's judgment and punishment of Israel as a necessary step to remove Israel's guilt. And Isaiah 27:2-6 reinterpreted Isaiah 5, the song of the vineyard, to reassure the Israelites in exile that God's judgment against them would be reversed and the Israelites would once again thrive in Israel. However, God's punishment of the Israelites would remain until their punishment was complete.

Second, the need for new leadership in Israel outside the succession of kings was prophesied by First Isaiah, because Israel's leaders were disobedient and corrupt. God would replace Israel's leaders with completely incapable leaders in Isaiah 3:4 "⁴I will make boys their princes, and babes shall rule over them." In addition, First Isaiah prophesied that the change in leadership could not come from within the succession of Israel's kings. Isaiah 9:1ff described Israel's new leader as someone who would bring about the righteous reign of a Messianic ruler. Some of the characteristics of the new leader are described in Isaiah 11:2 "²The spirit of the LORD shall rest on him [Immanuel], the spirit of wisdom and understanding, the spirit of counsel and might, the spirit of knowledge and the fear of the LORD." For Christian believers, Isaiah's prophecy of a new leader outside the succession of kings was actualized in the birth of Jesus, the Christ [the Messiah.]

Third, the re-creation of the people of God took place during Israel's exile in Babylon. Israel's independent kingship ended in their defeat by Babylon. In prophetic literature, the first prophet, Amos, introduced the idea of God being gracious to a faithful, repentant, remnant in Israel in Amos 5:15. But First Isaiah developed the idea of a faithful, repentant, remnant much further in Isaiah 10:21-22 "[21]A remnant will return, the remnant of Jacob, to God. [22]For though your people Israel were like the sand of the sea [Genesis 22:17], only a remnant of them will return." Isaiah further prophesied in Isaiah 1:9 "[9]If the LORD of hosts had not left us a few survivors [a remnant], we would have been like Sodom, and become like Gomorrah." First Isaiah prophesied that the returning faithful, repentant, obedient, remnant would live in peace, Isaiah 32:18, and an eschatological assembly of the nations of the world would gather at the sacred mountain of the Lord's house in Isaiah 2:2-4. Israel's new homeland would be ruled by a messianic king in Isaiah 33:17 in a new messianic society in Isaiah 11:10-12, which would eventually include all of creation, because the earth would be filled with the knowledge of God. God's presence and love would return to Israel and the world, because Israel would return to her original design of being a light to the nations and a witness to the glory of God.

Fourth, the necessary political changes to accomplish a new exodus from Babylon to Israel happened around

539 BCE, King Cyrus of Persia [modern day Iran] defeated the Babylonian Empire and became the major power in the Ancient Near East [ANE.] For Judeo-Christian believers, God commissioned King Cyrus of Persia to free the Israelites from Babylon and to help them rebuild the cities of Judah in Isaiah 44:24–45:25. Isaiah 44:28 also assured the Israelites that the foundation of their new temple would be laid.

Fifth, the necessary theological changes to accomplish the rebirth of the chosen people of God were prophesied by a new prophet, Second Isaiah in Isaiah 40–55. God will end Israel's punishment and the exiles will be comforted and allowed to return home to Israel in Isaiah 40:1 "¹Comfort, O comfort my people, says your God." Second Isaiah described the new leader that God would bring to Israel. He will be a chosen servant, on whom God's spirit will rest in Isaiah 42:1-4. He will bring about the salvation of Israel and justice to the nations. Second Isaiah introduced four suffering servant songs including Isaiah 42:1-4; 49:1-6; 50:4-9; 52:13–53:12, which describe the new Messiah as God's suffering servant and he described the servant's mission in Isaiah 49:6.

Who is God's suffering servant? The identity of the suffering servant of God is an ongoing scholarly theological debate. Most scholars agree that the first suffering servant song Isaiah 42:1-4 points to the nation of Israel as the suffering servant. The second suffering servant song Isaiah 49:1-6 also points to the nation of Israel as the suffering servant but leaves open the possibility of the servant being an individual, who is the embodiment of the nation of Israel. The third and fourth suffering servant songs in Isaiah 50:4-9 and 52:13-53:12 strongly point to an unknown individual, who for some Jewish believers may have lived during Second Isaiah's historical time. However, for Christian believers, Jesus is the actualization of the Isaiah's suffering servant in Mark 10:45 and Matthew 20:28.

What is the suffering servant's mission? The servant's mission is described in Isaiah 49:6 "It is too light a thing that you should be my servant to raise up the tribes of Jacob and to restore the survivors of Israel; I will give you as a light to the nations, that my salvation may reach to the end of the earth." The suffering servant will be a teacher, who sustains the weary through God's Word in Isaiah 50:4-5.

Sixth, the return to Israel of a re-created, faithful, repentant, obedient, remnant of the people of God would be made possible through the innocent suffering of God's vicarious suffering servant, who would give his life in order for God to release the guilt of His chosen people. God's judgment and punishment was complete, and God's presence and love would again shine through His chosen people.

In the fourth re-creation narrative, God's presence and love for humanity continued to evolve. God would no longer tolerate disobedience and idolatry from His chosen people; so, God re-created a faithful, repentant, obedient, remnant of the people of God. In addition, Isaiah prophesied that the nations would gather in Jerusalem and praise a new Messiah, who would not be from the succession of kings in Israel. However, Judaism never became a missionary religion [the book of Jonah is an exception], because there was no general acceptance of the suffering servant's mission or the unconditional inclusion of Gentiles into the kingdom [reign] of God. For Christian believers, Jesus is the actualization of Isaiah's vicarious suffering servant and in my opinion, Christianity became the necessary missionary extension of the people of God.

The Fifth Creation Narrative

In the fifth creation narrative, the relationship between God and humanity evolved significantly further for Christian believers, because Jesus is the fullest revelation of God's presence and love. We learn that Jesus is God in John 1:1-2 "¹In the beginning was the Word, and the Word was with God, and the Word was God. ²He [Jesus] was in the beginning with God." We find another biblical creation narrative in John 1:3 "³All things came into being through him [Jesus], and without him not one thing came into being." We learn that God became incarnate [human] in the person of

Jesus Christ in John 1:14 "¹⁴And <u>the Word became flesh</u> and lived among us, and we have seen his glory, the glory as of a father's only son, full of grace and truth." God's presence and love in our lives became most fully realized in Jesus Christ, because an encounter with Jesus is an encounter with God's presence and love. In Jesus' baptism (Mark 1:11; Matthew 3:17; Luke 3:22) and in Jesus' Transfiguration (Mark 9:7; Matthew 17:5; Luke 9:35), God the Father taught us that Jesus is His Son and we need to listen to Him.

Jesus' baptism and transfiguration are Christological events, because they inform us about Jesus' identity. [Who do you say I am?] In addition, Jesus' revelations about His relationship with His Father also confirm who Jesus is (e.g., John 10:30 "³⁰The Father and I are one.") During His ministry, Jesus revealed many things about His Father's ongoing love for humanity and Jesus taught us how to strengthen our relationship with God (e.g., by finding a better righteousness in Matthew 5–7 and Luke 6:12-49), which will lead us to abundant life in John 10:10 in the present day and in eternity in John 17:3 and 1 John 5:20.

It is absolutely necessary for us to hear the Word of God, but on at least three occasions in the Gospels hearing the Word of God proved insufficient: <u>First</u>, in the Synoptic Gospels, when Jesus read from the scriptures and explained their meaning in His hometown, the home town folks were offended by His words in Mark 6:2-6 and Matthew 13:54-58 and in Luke's Gospel, the home town folks were so offended that they wanted to throw Jesus off a cliff in Luke 4:28-29; <u>Second</u>, in the parable of the Sower in Mark 4:1-20; Matthew 13:1-17; and Luke 8:4-18, Jesus described the Word of God being heard by people but being received very differently (e.g., some people received the Word with joy but the Word was not nurtured by them; so, it had weak roots and when trouble or persecution came they immediately fell away from the Word); and <u>Third</u> in Mark's Gospel in Mark 15:34 and in Matthew's Gospel in Matthew 27:46, Jesus died utterly alone: "My God, my God, why have you forsaken me?" Where were all the people who heard the Word of God during Jesus' ministry, especially, His apostles? We need to hear the Word of God, but we also need to continuously nourish the Word of God in our hearts (e.g., by becoming a self-for-others.)

What adjustments can we introduce into our daily lives to help us to understand, nourish, and sustain God's presence and love? I can identify at least four ways to help keep the Word of God active in our daily lives: <u>First</u>, we can remember that Jesus is the light of the world, who brings humanity the fullest revelation of God's presence and love; <u>Second</u>, we can remember that Jesus came into the world to testify to the truth in John 18:37 "[37b]For this I was born, and for this I came into the world, to testify to the truth." Jesus' truth is found throughout the Gospels (e.g., Jesus taught us how to find a better righteousness in Matthew's Sermon on the Mount in Matthew 5–7 and in Luke's Sermon on the Plain in Luke 6:12-49); <u>Third</u>, we can remember that Jesus came into the world to save humanity in John 3:17 "¹⁷Indeed, God did not send the Son into the world to condemn the world, but in order that the world might be saved through him"; and <u>Fourth</u> we can remember that Jesus taught us that He came into the world to give us abundant life in John 10:10. We can find abundant life now and in eternity, when we find a better righteousness in Matthew 5–7 and Luke 6:12-49.

<u>In the fifth creation narrative, God's presence and love evolved, because of the incarnation of Jesus</u>, the Son of God, because an encounter with Jesus is an encounter with God's presence and love. Jesus' revelations about His Father can be found in all twenty-seven books of the NT, especially in the Gospels. St. Paul testified to the evolution of God's presence and love for humanity through Israel's patriarchs in Romans 9:4-5 "⁴They are Israelites, and to them belong the adoption, the glory, the covenants, the giving of the law, the worship, and the promises; ⁵to them belong the patriarchs, and from them, according to the flesh, comes the Messiah, who is over all, God blessed forever. Amen." Jesus is the son of David in the line of Judah through Mother Mary and for Christian believers, Jesus is the Messiah, the Christ.

St. Paul gives us his most explicit reference that Jesus is God in Romans 9:5b "⁵ᵇwho [Jesus] is over all, God blessed forever. Amen."

The Sixth Re-Creation Narrative

In the sixth re-creation narrative, God's presence and love can be found in Jesus' revelation that we need to be born from above or re-created spiritually, because God is spirit in John 4:24. Jesus taught us how to increase God's presence and love in our lives in the wonderful narrative between Jesus and a Pharisee named Nicodemus in John 3:1-21. Nicodemus was a very religious man and a learned member of the Sanhedrin, but he came to Jesus searching for answers to the same questions that we have. Jesus told Nicodemus that he must be re-created to be in right relationship with God in Jeremiah 31:31-34; Ezekiel 11:19-20; 36:26-27; and 1 Peter 1:22-25. Nicodemus needed to be born from above in John 3:3 "³Very truly, I tell you, no one can see the kingdom [reign] of God without being born from above." Jesus didn't equivocate in His discussion with Nicodemus; Jesus didn't say that He should be born from above; instead, Jesus taught Nicodemus and us that we must be born from above [spiritually] in order to obtain a positive, loving, personal relationship with God and in order to find a better righteousness in Matthew 5:20; because God is spirit, in John 4:24.

Our spiritual re-creation brings us closer to God's presence and love because we are re-created in our spirit [not in our body], in our outlook, and in our perspective, which brings us into a deeper, personal, loving relationship with God through our renewed faith, trust, hope, and love. Our spiritual re-creation requires making some changes in our lives including: <u>First</u>, confessing our sins; <u>Second</u>, accepting God's forgiveness for our sins; <u>Third</u>, repenting [changing our lives]; and <u>Fourth</u>, performing the required penance for our sins. Our spiritual re-creation is the key to obtaining the better righteousness described in Matthew 5–7. For Catholics, the sacrament of baptism causes us to be reborn into Christ.[5] In addition, as young adults, Catholics renew their re-creation into Christ through the sacrament of confirmation. However, as adults, we still need to continually rededicate our lives to God in some way (e.g., receiving the sacraments of the Catholic Church, becoming a self-for-others.)

<u>In the sixth re-creation narrative</u>, <u>God's presence and love evolved</u> because of Jesus' revelation to Nicodemus and us that we need to be re-created spiritually. Jesus' instructions are repeated in the NT by the holy apostles Peter and Paul. <u>Peter told us that Christians have become a new creation</u> in 1 Peter 1:23 "²³You have been born anew, not of perishable but of imperishable

---

5 "Catechism of the Catholic Church," articles 1214, 1215, 1216

seed, through the living and enduring word of God." Paul told us that Christians become a new creation in 2 Corinthians 5:17 "¹⁷So if anyone is in Christ, there is a new creation: everything old has passed away; see, everything has become new!" Our enemies remain in our midst (e.g., chaos and evil) but now we're able to experience God's presence and love in a new spiritual way with a renewed assurance of God's promises to humanity (e.g., Hebrews 13:5b "I will never leave you or forsake you.")

The Seventh Re-Creation Narrative

In the seventh re-creation narrative, we experience our final re-creation process, our individual resurrection, which allows us to continue to participate in God's ongoing love story with humanity for eternity. This final re-creation is the closest loving personal relationship that we believe we can have with God. This is final step in the evolution of God's biblical creation/re-creation process and this step includes faithful, obedient, repentant, Jewish and Christians believers and everyone described in Acts 10:34-35. We will all be grafted onto the branches of the tree of life in Genesis 3:22-24, which St. Paul described in Romans 11:16-24.

In this final biblical re-creation narrative, my focus is on our individual resurrection. Later in my book, I will discuss the kingdom [reign] of God, but first we need to examine the final creation narrative from two different perspectives: <u>first</u>, the OT view of our individual resurrection in Proverbs 12:28; Daniel 12:1-2; Isaiah 25:6-8; 26:19; and Psalm 49:15 and <u>second</u>, the NT view of our individual resurrection in John 11:25-27 and 1 Corinthians 15:35-58.

The OT View of Our Individual Resurrection

First temple Judaism [ca. 900–587 BCE] didn't generally accept the idea of the dead being individually resurrected. The idea of individual resurrection became more accepted in Jewish theology sometime after the second temple was completed [ca. 515 BCE.] So, in Jesus' day, many Pharisees believed in individual resurrection (e.g., St. Paul.) The Sadducees didn't accept individual resurrection, because they believed that it wasn't stated in the Pentateuch. During his ministry, Jesus refuted the Sadducees view of individual resurrection and he told the Sadducees that they didn't understand their own scriptures, in Mark 12:24-27 and Matthew 22:29-33. In my opinion, individual resurrection can be found in several OT verses (e.g., in Proverbs 12:28 "In the path of righteousness there is life, in walking its path there is no death" and Job 19:25-27 "For I know that my Redeemer lives, and that at the last he will stand upon the earth; and after my skin has been thus destroyed, then in my flesh I shall see God, whom I shall see on my side, and my eyes shall behold, and not another.

My heart faints within me!") There are additional references to individual resurrection in the Apocrypha in 2 Maccabees. 7:13 and Wisdom 3:1-9.

In my opinion, the most specific OT reference to individual resurrection is in the book of Daniel [ca. 164 BCE.] Daniel prophesied that individual resurrection would occur after the persecution that accompanies the eschaton in Daniel 12:2 "²Many of those who sleep in the dust of the earth shall awake, some to everlasting life, and some to shame and everlasting contempt." Daniel was told to seal his book in Daniel 8:26 until the time of the final crises, which the book of Daniel anticipated would occur when his book was written (ca. 164 BCE.) In the book of Revelation [ca. 100 CE], John of Patmos was given the opposite message about sealing his book, in Revelation 22:10 "¹⁰And he said to me, 'Do not seal up the words of the prophecy of this book, for the time is near...'" Despite the hopes and optimism of the authors of the books of Daniel and Revelation and the apocalyptic chapters of the Synoptic Gospels, Jesus was very clear that only the Father knows when the eschaton will occur, in Mark 13:32 and Matthew 24:36.

The NT View of Individual Resurrection

The NT view of individual resurrection is described in at least two ways: <u>first</u>, Jesus' resurrection from the dead, which gives Christians the hope of their own individual resurrection and <u>second</u>, St. Paul describes the necessary changes to our humanity in order to be individually resurrected in 1 Corinthians 15:35-58.

First, for Christian believers, Jesus is the only authoritative figure who can speak about individual resurrection, because Christians believe that He's the only one, who rose from the dead. The Synoptic Gospels describe many examples of Jesus prophesying about His death and resurrection, in Mark 8:31; 9:30-31;10:32-34; Matthew 16:21; 17:22-23; 20:18-19; and Luke 9:21-22; 17:20-37; 18:31-33. The Gospel narratives also provide details about Jesus' resurrection appearances (e.g., Jesus appeared to His apostle, Thomas, in John 20:24-29; Jesus appeared to two disciples on the road to Emmaus in Luke 24:13-35; and Jesus appeared to many of his disciples in Luke 24:36-49.) St. Paul summarized Jesus' resurrection appearances in 1 Corinthians 15:3-8. The Christian hope of our own individual resurrection is very much alive, because Christians believe that Jesus is very much alive. In the narrative about the death of Lazarus, Jesus talked to Martha about resurrection, in John 11:25-27 "[25]Jesus said to her, 'I am the resurrection and the life. Those who believe in me, even though they die, will live, [26]and everyone who lives and believes in me will never die. Do you believe this?' [27]She said to him, 'Yes, Lord, I believe that you are the Messiah, the Son of God, the one coming into the world.'"

Second, in my opinion, St. Paul provides a wonderful description of what has to change in order for us to be individually resurrected into the kingdom [reign] of God. St. Paul's theology of resurrection begins with an acknowledgment that Jesus was resurrected in 1 Corinthians 15:20, 24-26 "[20]But in fact Christ has been raised from the dead, the first fruits of those who have died...[24]Then comes the end, when he hands over the kingdom to God the Father, after he has destroyed every ruler and every authority and power. [25]For he must reign until he has put all his enemies under his feet. [26]The last enemy to be destroyed is death." For Christian believers, we will be individually resurrected. In his second extant letter to the Corinthians, St. Paul described the Christian hope of becoming a new creation in Christ in 2 Corinthians 5:17 "[17]So if anyone is in Christ, there is a new creation: everything old has passed away; see, everything has become new!"

Jesus revealed the necessary preparation for transformation into resurrected life in John 12:24-25 "[24]Very truly, I tell you, unless a grain of wheat falls into the earth and dies, it remains just a single grain; but if it dies, it bears much fruit. [25]Those who love their life lose it, and those who hate their life in this world will keep it for eternal life." St. Paul teaches us that during our lives we are gradually being prepared for our transformation into the kingdom of God, in 2 Corinthians 3:18 "[18]And all of us, with unveiled faces, seeing the glory of the Lord as though reflected in a mirror, are being transformed into the same image from one degree of glory to another;

for this comes from the Lord, the Spirit." However, St. Paul goes significantly further in 1 Corinthians 15:35-58, as he describes the necessary physical changes to accomplish our individual resurrection into a new creation. In my opinion, St. Paul follows Jesus' teaching in John 12:24-25 in describing that our existing bodies as a seed that must die in order to be sown into a new creation, that is, in order to be fully transformed into our resurrected bodies.

St. Paul identified four physical differences between our current bodies and our resurrected bodies in 1 Corinthians 15:42-44 "[42a]So it is with the resurrection of the dead." First, "[42b]What is sown is perishable, what is raised is imperishable."; Second, "[43]It is sown in dishonor, it is raised in glory."; Third, "It is sown in weakness, it is raised in power'"; and Fourth, "[44]It is sown a physical body, it is raised a spiritual body." For St. Paul, our present human existence and our resurrected human existence are radically different, and God is the source and power of this necessary final re-creation in 1 Corinthians 15:50 "[50]What I am saying, brothers and sisters, is this: flesh and blood cannot inherit the kingdom [reign] of God, nor does the perishable inherit the imperishable." St. Paul conflated two OT texts Hosea 13:14 and Isaiah 25:8 into a single citation to illustrate how our victory over death is achieved through Jesus Christ, in 1 Corinthians 15:54-57 "[54]When this perishable body puts on imperishability, and this mortal body puts on immortality, then the saying that is written will be fulfilled: 'Death has been swallowed up in victory. [55]Where, O death, is your victory? Where, O death, is your sting?' [56]The sting of death is sin, and the power of sin is the law. [57]But thanks be to God, who gives us the victory through our Lord Jesus Christ."

In the seventh re-creation narrative, God's love becomes eternally present for those who inherit the kingdom [reign] of God in Romans 8:14-17. Through the power of God, we will be transformed and re-created into an imperishable spiritual body, which will be raised in power and glory to an eternal life in God's presence and love. This was God's original design and plan for His most glorious creation, humanity, in Wisdom 2:23a "[23]for God created us for incorruption, and made us in the image of his own eternity." God's original intentions for humanity were established in the first creation narrative in Genesis 1:26-27 and for Christian believers, God's intentions come to fruition in the seventh re-creation narrative.

CHAPTER TWO

Finding God's Presence and Love in God's Theocentric Creation

Introduction

In chapter one of my book, I described God's faithful enduring presence and love throughout an evolutionary seven-step biblical creation/re-creation process. In chapter two, I'm asking a fundamental design question about God's creation: did God design His creation for humanity (e.g., an anthropocentric creation) or did God design His creation for God (e.g., a theocentric creation)? Humanity tends to see the world from an anthropocentric perspective, because God gave humanity dominion over His creation in Genesis 1:26, 28. But what if the world over which humanity was given dominion was designed by God for God? What if

God created and designed a theocentric creation? If God designed His creation for God, then we need to change our perspective on how God's creation works in Isaiah 55:8-9 "⁸For my thoughts are not your thoughts, nor are your ways my ways, says the LORD. ⁹For as the heavens are higher than the earth, so are my ways higher than your ways and my thoughts than your thoughts."

My question about the fundamental design of God's creation is answered in the wonderful book of Job, where we find God's presence and love through the struggles of an innocent man named Job. In some sense, Job is a proxy for humanity, because Job is searching for answers to the same questions that we are searching for answers. In this biblical narrative, Job's life is instantaneously and dramatically changed (e.g., Job went from being wealthy to being poor), because of a wager in heaven between God and Satan [the accuser, not the devil.] The purpose of the heavenly wager was to determine whether Job was a righteous man because of his nature or because of his current well-to-do situation. Throughout the narrative, Job is very unhappy with the unwelcome changes to his life. Eventually, Job accuses God of two things: First, God did a poor job designing His creation (e.g., God used His wisdom to create chaos in nature and society instead of creating order in nature and society in Job 12:13-25) and Second, God deals unjustly with His creation, in Job

9:19-35; 19:7-12. At the end of the narrative, God visits Job in a theophany and makes two speeches to Job in Job 38–41, which correspond to Job's two accusations. God's speeches challenge Job [and us] to understand the underlying design of God's creation, especially the mysteries found in its many incongruities.

<u>In God's first speech, He addresses Job's first accusation that God did a poor job designing His creation in Job 38:1–40:2.</u> God questioned Job's understanding of the design of His creation in Job 38:4 "⁴Where were you when I laid the foundation of the earth? Tell me, if you have understanding." But Job wasn't present when God laid the foundation of the earth, so he doesn't know how creation occurred. Next, God asked Job a series of technical questions about the design of creation in order to further test Job's understanding of the design of God's creation: <u>First, what is Job's understanding of the structural elements in God's creation</u> (e.g., has Job seen the invisible recesses of the deep or the gates of death in Job 38:16-17 or the movements of the least perceptible star in the galaxy in Job 38:31-33); <u>Second, what is Job's understanding of the more practical elements in God's creation</u> (e.g., can Job explain the providential care that God has for His creation (e.g., bringing rain and grass where no one lives in Job 38:24-27 and providing food for the prey and the predator in Job 38:39-40); and <u>Third</u>, does Job understand how God

controls the waters of chaos, Job 38:8 "who shut in the sea with doors when it burst out from the womb?" The answer to God's questions must be: <u>God alone did this</u>. God's implied answer resonates with the trial speeches in Isaiah 40:12ff; 41:28-29; 43:8-15; 44:6ff; 45:20-25, when YHWH confronted the gods of the nations in a legal battle to determine who is truly God, which led to the same conclusion as the book of Job: <u>God alone is God</u>.

<u>God asked Job about his understanding of the living creatures in His creation</u> (e.g., does Job understand the mysteries of the animal kingdom, because humanity has not domesticated most of the animals in creation, but God still provides for them every day?) God asked Job to demonstrate how he would provide nutrition for the wild creatures living everywhere in His creation, who God feeds daily in Job 38:39-41 "[39]Can you hunt the prey for the lion, or satisfy the appetite of the young lions, [40]when they crouch in their dens, or lie in wait in their covert [hidden cave?] [41]Who provides for the raven its prey, when its young ones cry to God, and wander about for lack of food?" According to the California Academy of Sciences, there are 6.5 million species of life on land and 2.2 million species of life in the oceans. In my opinion, the majority of living species in God's inscrutable creation get along fine without human help in a world where the cycle of death is balanced daily against the cycle of life in Job 38:17 and in Job 39:1-6.

In God's second speech, God addresses Job's second accusation that He deals unjustly with His creation in Job 40:6–41:34. God challenged Job's underlying assumption that human beings are at the center of the universe, because God created the world for God, not for humanity (e.g., humanity isn't mentioned in God's two speeches to Job.) God is just as concerned about the wastelands He created as He is about the rest of His creation, in Job 38:25-27, 36-38.

God's creation includes the symbols of chaos: First, Behemoth, a land monster in Job 40:15ff and Second, Leviathan, a sea monster in Job 41. So, chaos exists within God's design, because Behemoth and Leviathan are important to God; however, they exist within God's design constraints, in Job 40:15-24 and Job 41:1-34. By contrast, Job can neither control nor eliminate the forces of chaos in the world. God's responses to Job seem to indicate that in a world full of mysterious incongruities there are no simple answers to what appears to be innocent suffering (e.g., a baby eagle survives because another creature dies.) The book of Job suggests that some of the suffering and incongruities in God's creation are not evil; rather, they are a divine mystery.

It's a lot easier to find God's presence and love in our lives when our starting point is that God created the world for God, not for humanity. In his book *Beyond*

Good and Evil, Friedrich Nietzsche explained how to obtain freedom by eliminating morality; however, in my opinion, freedom can never be obtained in an immoral world. Freedom is God's gift that allows us to love God, self, and others. If Nietzsche was trying to escape the theological reward-punishment doctrine, then his efforts were in vain, because God's justice and mercy can never be limited to a specific theological doctrine. That would make God predictable and put the Absolute Mystery of God in a box, which we do not have the power to do. Instead, we need to reevaluate our understanding of God's creation and make room for the incongruities and mysteries that we find daily, because God designed them into His creation for God's mysterious purposes.

In my opinion, we live in a world that is intentionally created and designed by God for God, not for humanity, a world that is permeated with the offer of grace [God's presence and love] from the beginning of creation. Our conclusion should be, why would I settle for the pleasures of the secular world when I can find a better righteousness through Jesus' teaching (e.g., in the Sermon on the Mount in Matthew 5–7) and I can find the abundant life that Jesus came to reveal to us (in John 10:10.)

The book of Ecclesiastes also reminds us how little we know about God's creation, in Ecclesiastes 11:5 "[5]Just as you do not know how the breath comes to the bones in the mother's womb, so you do not know the work of God, who makes everything." Our restlessness (e.g., our unending questions) necessarily drive us to search for God's presence and love, even though some of the answers will remain with the Absolute Mystery of God, in Job. 38–41.

Part Two:
Finding God's Presence and Love through Theological Conditions

Introduction

<u>In part one of my book</u>, I described God's presence and love for humanity in an evolutionary seven-step biblical creation process. And even though humanity was given dominion over God's creation in Genesis 1:26, 28, I described the design of God's creation as theocentric, not anthropocentric. In each of the seven biblical creation/re-creation narratives, I examined God's evolving relationship with humanity; however, I didn't address humanity's need to be in relationship with God. But we're created and designed by God to be in a positive, loving, personal relationship with Him. Therefore, we need to understand how to communicate with God through His offer of grace, and we need to understand how God communicates with us through the same method. My definition of the word grace is: "God's presence and love." For Christian believers, I'm describing God's amazing grace.

<u>God's offer of grace provides the necessary underlying wiring to connect humanity with divinity</u>. However, like the electricity wired into our homes and businesses, we need to turn on a switch to activate the electricity. Similarly, we need to consciously and freely accept God's offer of grace to enable, develop, and sustain a positive, loving, personal relationship with God and bring His presence and love more deeply into our lives. For Christian believers, the Word of God

became incarnate [human] in John 1:14 "¹⁴And the Word became flesh and lived among us, and we have seen his glory, the glory as of a father's only son, <u>full of grace and truth</u>." Jesus is the source of our strength and hope. St. Paul described the impact of God's grace on him in Philippians 4:13 "¹³I can do all things through him [Jesus] who strengthens me."

Part two of my book builds on part one, with my belief that God created and designed us to be in a positive, loving, personal relationship with Him – but how do we accomplish that? God's unmerited gift of the offer of grace is how God communicates to us all day every day, and our acceptance of God's offer of grace is how we communicate with God. My book describes God's offer of grace to humanity from three different perspectives: <u>First</u>, the human perspective coming to the intersection of humanity and divinity, God's offer of grace; <u>Second</u>, the actual intersection of humanity and divinity, God's offer of grace; and <u>Third</u> the divine perspective coming to the intersection of divinity and humanity, God's offer of grace.

We begin by examining the human side of the intersection of humanity and divinity. In chapter three, I examine foundational theological conditions [existentials] that make us different from other beings (e.g. our self-presence) and I examine additional theological conditions that make us different from other beings (e.g., the seeds of our many gifts from God.)

CHAPTER THREE

The Human Theological Conditions Necessary to Accept God's Offer of Grace

The Foundational Theological Conditions Necessary to Find and Accept God's Offer of Grace

My foundational theological conditions are based on my understanding of Karl Rahner's theological anthropology. The pluralized titles of Rahner's first two books help us to understand Rahner's theology: we're "Spirits in the World" designed to be "Hearers of the Word." The foundational theological conditions that make us different from other beings are described throughout Rahner's theological anthropology.[6] Rahner focused on four conditions [existentials] that

---
6 Karl Rahner SJ, "Foundations of Christian Faith," 117-133

allow us to develop and sustain a relationship with God by accepting His offer of grace in our everyday lives. However, additional theological conditions [existentials] could certainly be added to Rahner's preliminary foundational list. "The word 'existential' (borrowed from Heidegger) indicates an aspect of human life, a reality of existence."[7] Rahner's four conditions [existentials] include: <u>First</u>, self-presence, <u>Second</u>, self-transcendence, <u>Third</u>, the supernatural existential [God's offer of grace], and <u>Fourth,</u> freedom.

<u>Rahner's first condition [existential] is called self-presence</u>. Through our gift of self-presence, we not only know, we know that we know. Our conscious awareness of ourselves [self-presence] is much more than the sum of our parts, despite the efforts of the empirical sciences (e.g., sociology, genetics) to explain humanity based on observing it. Human beings are more than an instance of humanity rolled off an assembly line. We need a better understanding of ourselves than we can find in the empirical sciences of post-modernity, because human beings surpass in complexity and mystery the sum of their parts. We are uniquely created by God, in Genesis 1:27; 2:7; Jeremiah 1:5; and Psalm 139:16; therefore, we're radically dependent on God for our existence and our fulfillment. In my opinion, we have a designed orientation toward God and a designed trajectory toward God to help us return home to God.

---

[7] Thomas F. O'Meara, "God in the World," 59

Rahner's second condition [existential] is called self-transcendence. Our gift of self-transcendence facilitates the way we learn, because our everyday sense experience occurs within the transcendent horizon of the Absolute Mystery God in whom we are grounded. We move toward God's offer of grace through our gift of self-transcendence, because it's God's gift that turns finite human beings into spiritual human beings, who are capable of a glimpse of God even though we know that God is much more than we've grasped. Our everyday transcendent experience is not an out of body experience, because we're spirits in the world who can communicate with God, who is Spirit, in John 4:24. Indeed, it is through our self-transcendence and God's divine nature in John 4:24 that we're drawn into being and become capable of sharing God's offer of grace in at least two ways: <u>First</u>, <u>unthematically</u>, that is, we're not necessarily aware of being in God's presence and love and <u>Second</u>, <u>asymptotically</u>, that is, we experience God's presence and love in a way similar to the behavior of a mathematical asymptote [no matter how many times we divide the distance between the curve and the line we can never approach the line.] And no matter how much we try to understand God's presence and love in our lives, we lack the capacity to fully understand the Absolute Mystery of God. More importantly, through our self-transcendence, we know that we don't control either the source or the ground of our everyday experience, because we know that our everyday experience occurs within a broader horizon.

<u>Rahner's third condition [existential] is called the supernatural existential</u>. This is the broader horizon that we experience in our everyday transcendence. Through "the supernatural existential" God grasps us, because we're spirits in the world designed to hear God's Word. "A supernatural existential is a form not phenomenologically seen but held by faith to be real and present, present in every person at least in the mode of an offer."[8] What St. Thomas Aquinas called "the more," Rahner calls the "supernatural existential." We may be unaware that our everyday experience occurs in God's presence and love, because God is unthematically present to us, or we may be aware that we're in God's presence and love, because God is thematically present to us (e.g., when we read and study the Word of God or when we attend a religious service.) We remain free to refuse God's offer of grace. Regardless of our circumstances and choices, our everyday reality remains the same, because the Absolute Mystery of God cannot and does not disclose itself to us in the same way as sense experience discloses an object to us, because God is not an object, in John 4:24. God's presence and love is radically rooted in the depths of our consciousness, but it can be suppressed. In my experience, the offer

---

8 Thomas F. O'Meara, "God in the World," 59

of grace still breaks into our lives at critical moments, sometimes thematically, sometimes unthematically, but always asymptotically.

Rahner's fourth condition [existential] is called freedom. Our gift of human freedom is another name for our spirituality. Theologically, freedom provides us with the ability to love and to be loved, because our freedom gives us the capacity to consider the other. However, our freedom is finite; it operates within God's infinite divine freedom and not next to God's infinite divine freedom. Our freedom allows us to enter a relationship and surrender ourselves to another in love. If we disregard our freedom to love, then we fail to love and be loved. For me, our freedom was pragmatically and philosophically expressed by Marcus Aurelius [121-180 CE] in his *Meditations*: "Our life is what our thoughts make it." The corollary to Marcus Aurelius' observation is that we can be in God's presence and love by accepting and animating God's offer of grace in our thoughts and in our lives. In John's Gospel, Jesus revealed how to use our freedom in a more theological way, when He assured His disciples that they will find peace in Him, in John 17:27 "[27]Peace I leave with you; my peace I give to you. I do not give to you as the world gives. Do not let your hearts be troubled, and do not let them be afraid." God's presence and love is always available to us, but we must accept God's offer of grace through our freedom. For Rahner, "Our self-actualization standing before God through knowing (which constitutes our nature as spirit) possesses, as an intrinsic element of this knowledge, a love for God. Our love for God is not something that may happen or not happen, once we have come to know God. As an intrinsic element of knowledge, it is both its condition and its ground."[9]

Our freedom gives us the capacity to love God, self, and others. Our freedom also gives us the capacity to refuse to believe in or love God, which leads humanity to substituting a counterfeit God for the real God, in Romans 1:19-25. Our freedom is a condition [an existential] in our foundational theological nature and God's offer of grace doesn't crowd out our freedom.

Additional Theological Conditions Necessary to Accept God's Offer of Grace

Introduction

Rahner's foundational theological conditions [existentials] help us to understand the basic differences between human beings and other beings. However, God enhances our theological human design by including the seeds of many different kinds of gifts (e.g., the ability to sing.) These additional conditions are added to our human design and they help us to develop a better righteousness, in Matthew 5:20, and to lead us to an encounter with God's presence and love.

---
9 Karl Rahner SJ, "Hearer of the Word," 81

However, we're not born fully mature nor are our gifts given to us fully mature. We need to nurture the seeds of all our gifts (e.g., through education and application) in order to bring them to maturity. We need to examine and understand our more complete theological human design by using the background biblical metaphor of the potter and the clay. The Creator molds the clay according to His purposes, but God's divine purposes remain hidden and mysterious to humans In Deuteronomy 29:29 "The secret things belong to the LORD our God, but the revealed things belong to us and to our children forever, to observe all the words of this law."

God's gifts make us different from other beings

What kinds of gifts are we given by God? We're born with the seeds of at least six different kinds of gifts, which makes God's presence and love accessible to help us develop and sustain a positive, loving, personal relationship with God: <u>First</u>, our unique individual gifts, <u>Second,</u> the gift of time, <u>Third</u>, the gift of the scriptures, <u>Fourth</u>, the gift of virtues, <u>Fifth</u>, the gift of abstraction, and <u>Sixth</u> the gift of restlessness.

<u>The first gift that makes God's love present to us is the seeds of our unique individual gifts</u> (e.g., academic gifts, artistic gifts, athletic gifts, and spiritual gifts.) We need to nourish and develop our unique gifts,

because they're perishable and because together with our other gifts they're designed to lead us to a better righteousness that will help us to become a self-for-others.

<u>The second gift that makes God's love present to us is the gift of time</u>. We're given the gift of life, but it comes with an unknown expiration date; therefore, time is a precious gift from God. Jesus understood the gift of time, when He taught us how to pray to His Father "give us this day our daily bread." And the psalmist understood God's gift of time in Psalm 139:16 "[16]Your eyes beheld my unformed substance. <u>In your book were written all the days that were formed for me</u>, when none of them yet existed." Unfortunately, we don't have access to God's book, so we don't know our expiration date. Therefore, we need to spend the time that we're given using our many gifts to develop a better righteousness, which leads to a positive, loving, personal relationship with God (e.g., helping others through our own unique ministries.) Jesus gave us countless examples of how people foolishly spend their time (e.g., in the parable of the Rich Fool, in Luke 12:16-21, we learn about a man who tore down his barns to build bigger barns for his anticipated excess, but his life was taken from him before he could accumulate the additional wealth he sought.)

We need to accomplish what God wants us to accomplish in the time that we are given (e.g., we need to find a ministry that helps others), because it's God's time; it's not our time. In order to find and nurture a ministry that helps others, we need to get past our pride, our mistakes, our fear of failure, our disobedience, our laziness, and we need to obey God's commandments. The time will come when we cannot serve God or others, so we need to do it now as St. Paul reminds us in 2 Corinthians 6:2 "See, now is the acceptable time; see, now is the day of salvation!" We need to use the time we are given knowing that we are adopted children of God, in Romans 8:15, 23; 9:4; Galatians 4:5; and Ephesians 1:5-6. There is one more critical element in God's gift of time, that is, time changes us. Hopefully, we are given sufficient time to accept God's offer of grace and find our way home to God.

<u>The third gift that makes God's love present to us is the gift of the Judeo-Christian Bible, the Word of God, which gives us a divine blueprint on how to live our lives.</u> The Word of God makes God's presence and love externally and permanently available to us in print and in the message of God's ministers, in Isaiah 40:8 "[8]The grass withers, the flower fades; but the word of our God will stand forever." The scriptures awe us, inspire us, comfort us, protect us, and guide us to finding a better righteousness (e.g., in Matthew 6:10, 'Your will be done.") St. Paul described the treasures that await us when we find God's presence and love in our lives in 1 Corinthians 2:9-10 "[9]But, as it is written, 'What no eye

has seen, nor ear heard, nor the human heart conceived, what God has prepared for those who love him' – [10]these things God has revealed to us through the Spirit; for the Spirit searches everything, even the depths of God." The Word of God in the scriptures makes God's offer of grace immediately and thematically present to us, unlike our daily transcendent unthematic experiences of God's offer of grace. Isaiah described how the Word of God impacts our lives in Isaiah 55:10-11 "[10]For as the rain and the snow come down from heaven, and do not return there until they have watered the earth, making it bring forth and sprout, giving seed to the Sower and bread to the eater, [11]so shall my word be that goes out from my mouth; it shall not return to me empty, but it shall accomplish that which I purpose, and succeed in the thing for which I sent it." I will say more about the marvelous gift of scriptures later in my book.

We need to reevaluate our everyday circumstances as we study the scriptures (e.g., we do not create wealth on our own, because the gold and silver belong to God, who makes people wealthy so they can help others.) There are many scriptural and non-scriptural examples that teach us to share our gifts with others (e.g., <u>First</u>, 1 Peter 4:10 "[10]Like good stewards of the manifold grace of God, serve one another with whatever gift each of you has received"; and <u>Second</u>, in Matthew's Gospel we learn how God treated the laborers in the vineyard in Matthew 20:1-16; we learn that God's way of sharing does not conform to humanity's way of sharing, because Isaiah teaches us how God works in Isaiah 55:8-9 "⁸For my thoughts are not your thoughts, nor are your ways my ways, says the LORD. ⁹For as the heavens are higher than the earth, so are my ways higher than your ways and my thoughts than your thoughts."

The fourth gift that makes God's love present to us is the seeds of several kinds of virtues. We begin with a definition of virtue: "Virtue is a habitual and firm disposition to do good."¹⁰ St. Paul established many Christian communities, and he emphasized practicing virtues within these communities, because virtues build up and sustain communities, in 1 Corinthians 12:4-11; Romans 12:3-8, whereas vices tear down and destroy communities. Humans are given the seeds of at least three kinds of virtues including: First, the cardinal virtues; Second, the relational virtues; and Third, the theological virtues.

First, the seeds of the four cardinal virtues are inchoate, that is, they're in our DNA. The cardinal virtues were originally introduced into western civilization by the Greek philosophers some twenty-five hundred years ago (e.g., in the writings of Plato) and they were subsequently incorporated into Christianity. There are four cardinal virtues including: First, prudence, which guides our judgment and gives us the ability to

---

10 "Catechism of the Catholic Church," article 1833

discipline ourselves to do the right thing in our everyday lives; <u>Second</u>, <u>fortitude</u>, which gives us the courage we need to confront pain or adversity in our everyday lives; <u>Third</u>, <u>temperance</u>, which guides us to moderate our everyday actions by exercising self-restraint in Titus 2:11-13; and <u>Fourth</u>, <u>justice</u>, which guides us to give God His due and to be reasonable and fair in dealing with our neighbors.

<u>Second</u>, the seeds of the cardinal virtues nurture our individual development. For Jim Keenan SJ, and others, we also need to nurture our relational virtues, because we live our lives in community. The relational virtues help us to increase our sense of responsibility for each other. The relational virtues include but are not limited to: mercy, hospitality, gratitude, sympathy, reconciliation, and humor.

<u>Third</u>, the seeds of our theological virtues [faith, hope, and love] help us to find and secure our relationship with God. The theological virtues are discussed later in my book.

<u>The fifth gift that makes God's love present to us is the gift of abstraction, or our ability to understand ideas beyond events (e.g., we are able to grasp a universal idea from a particular object.</u>) In other words, we're capable of knowing something independent of the attributes of a given object. It is through our gift of abstraction that we can find God's presence and love in our everyday transcendent experience, because we know that a

particular object has limitations and we also know that the essence of a particular object is unlimited (e.g., in sensing a specific chair we are limited to the specific chair, but the idea of chairs is unlimited.) So, the gift of abstraction reveals the possibility of "limitlessness," which is a phenomenon written about throughout the history of philosophy and theology.

For Judeo-Christian believers, God's presence and love is the limitless horizon in which objects appear to us, and without this broader, limitless horizon simultaneously experienced in our sense experience we would be limited to the bounds of a specific object. There are many different ways to describe the phenomenon of limitlessness, but I'm only going to briefly mention seven descriptions: First, for Kant, our feeling of limitlessness is confined to the horizon of our sense experience, so our limitlessness is confined to space and time; Second, for Nietzsche, our limitlessness is the horizon of nothingness [a void]; Third, for Ernst Bloch, who was a German Marxist philosopher, our limitlessness is empty; Fourth, for St. Thomas Aquinas, our limitlessness is understood as "the more," which cannot be an object of the same kind, because it goes beyond the limits of a specific object; Fifth, for Karl Rahner SJ, we experience "the Vorgriff," which allows a single object to be understood within the horizon of all that can be understood. In the "Vorgriff," we experience God's offer of grace through the supernatural existential. Through the "Vorgriff," God's love becomes present to us in our transcendent experience as an offer of grace. <u>Sixth, for Bill Dych SJ</u>, during the process of knowing we exceed our grasp. We ask questions endlessly, because we know that we have not exhausted all the answers to our questions, which helps us understand our own finiteness. If we understand our everyday experience in the "Vorgriff," then we understand that we are in the presence of the Absolute Mystery of God. And, <u>Seventh, for Randy Sachs SJ</u>, Rahner understands God's Spirit as present "everywhere in particular." It's the Spirit within us that allows us to experience existence in transcendence.[11]

<u>The sixth gift that makes God's love present to us is the gift of restlessness.</u> The psalmist waited in silence for God's answers to him in Psalm 62:1 "'For God alone my soul waits in silence; from him comes my salvation." In his *Confessions*, St. Augustine understood the need for waiting for God in silence, but he went further and described the impact of our restlessness, while we are waiting for God: "You have made us for yourself, O Lord, and our hearts are restless until they rest in you."[12] Rahner developed the idea of restlessness significantly further than St. Augustine. For Rahner, the purpose of our restlessness is to drive us to an encounter with God.

---

[11] Randy Sachs SJ, "Karl Rahner, The legacy of Vatican II and its urgency for theology today," 33

[12] St. Augustine, *Confessions*

For Rahner, and I agree with Rahner, we necessarily search for God's presence and love in our everyday lives, because we're designed to search for God. Therefore, our search for God's presence and love manifests itself in various forms of restlessness (e.g., through our questions, through our dissatisfactions, through our inadequacies, through our loneliness, through our fears), because nothing in our experience measures up to God's presence and love in our innermost being. If we deny God's presence and love in our lives, then we place unrealistic expectations on the people and things that are present in our lives, because they can never fulfill all our needs.

The idea of restlessness is so critical to Rahner's theology that I want to make his point at the beginning of his theological career in his first doctoral dissertation *Spirit in the World*, Rahner explained that our restlessness (e.g., our questions) drives us to an encounter with God.

"Man questions. This is something final and irreducible. For in human existence the question is that fact which absolutely refuses to be replaced by another fact, to be reduced back to another fact and thus to be unmasked once again as being itself derivative and provisional... So, <u>the question is first the only "must," the only necessity</u>, the only thing beyond question to which questioning man is bound, the only circle in which his questioning is caught, the only apriority to which it is subject. <u>Man questions necessarily</u>."[13]

Sometime later in his career in *Foundations of Christian Faith*, Rahner repeated his insights about our restlessness (e.g., our questions.)

"Man is not the unquestioning and unquestioned infinity of reality. <u>He is the question which rises up before him, empty, but really and inescapably, and which can never be settled and never adequately answered by him.</u>"[14]

We can search for the person or thing that we think will give us what we want but we will eventually discover that it's not enough. The essence of sin is idolatry, that is, by elevating a person or a thing above God, we violate the first commandment, choose sin, and return to the prison of sin. "The God experience is the cause of our dissatisfaction with life, for nothing measures up to that which rests at our deepest center."[15] Through the intervention and help of the Holy Spirit, our restlessness drives us to an encounter with God, where we find God's offer of grace [God's presence and love], which liberates us from the prison of selfishness. Even though our restlessness drives us to an encounter with God's presence and love, we do not escape from

---

13   Karl Rahner SJ, *Spirit in the World*, 57

14   Karl Rahner SJ, *Foundations of Christian Faith*, 32

15   Harvey D. Egan SJ, Karl Rahner – Mystic of Everyday Life, 60

the world that we live in, including our emotions, temptations, dichotomies, incongruities, evil, and the fear of death.

For St. Thomas Aquinas, grace gives us a rudimentary union with God, which will be expanded in the beatific vision, that is, we will eventually experience a more direct communication with God as St. Paul describes in 1 Corinthains 13:12 "[12]For now we see in a mirror, dimly, but then we will see face to face. Now I know only in part; then I will know fully, even as I have been fully known." In the meantime, we need to remain open to God's presence and love in our everyday lives and circumstances (e.g., Moses warned the Israelites not to forget God in their prosperity in Deuteronomy 8:3 "[3]He humbled you by letting you hunger, then by feeding you with manna, with which neither you nor your ancestors were acquainted, in order to make you understand that one does not live by bread alone, but by every word that comes from the mouth of the LORD.") Christian believers should never forget the words of St. Paul to Christians or Moses' to the Israelites.

CHAPTER FOUR

The Theological Intersection Between Humanity and Divinity

Introduction

God's offer of grace is the intersection between humanity and divinity. My definition of grace is simply: "God's presence and love." I remind Christian believers that I'm attempting to describe God's <u>amazing grace</u>. For St. Thomas Aquinas, when we experience a chair, we also experience "the more," that is, we experience the broader horizon in which we experience the chair, which simultaneously informs us that there are numerous other chairs. This broader horizon that we experience in our everyday transcendence is what Rahner calls God's offer of grace or "the supernatural existential [condition]" through which God grasps us, because we're spirits in the world designed to hear God's Word. We access God's offer of grace through the Holy Spirit <u>externally</u> in the world and, for Christian believers, <u>internally</u> in our deepest being. We necessarily communicate with God spiritually, because God is Spirit, in John 4:24 "²⁴God is spirit, and those who worship God must worship God in spirit and truth."

God's steadfast faithful love grounds the source, the horizon, and the fulfillment of our everyday existence. For Roger Haight SJ, in the intersection of humanity and divinity we experience God's offer of grace: "<u>Grace is God as Spirit</u>, God's gift of self, which is at the same time a presence to, and implicitly a being active in, the human spirit or freedom that constitutes every person. And this grace, or God as Spirit, can be experienced and in fact is commonly experienced in this world."[16] It is important to recognize that God's offer of grace is available to us all day, every day, because God continually takes the initiative to communicate His presence and love to us.

The Theological Impact of God's Offer of Grace When Divinity Touches Humanity

Given that the offer of grace is the intersection of humanity and divinity, we need to understand the

---

16 Roger Haight SJ, *Jesus Symbol of God*, 452

impact of the offer of grace on our humanity, when we accept God's offer of grace. Although the word grace is rarely used explicitly in OT theology, God's chosen people certainly understood the impact of God's presence and love throughout their scriptures. The impact of God's offer of grace [God's presence and love] in the OT was to build up and sustain God's chosen people, especially in their theology of creation in Genesis 1:26; 12:1ff, in their theology of redemption in Exodus 1:15-22; Isaiah 40–55, and in their theology of salvation in Isaiah 37:36; 2 Kings 19:35.

The Impact of Grace on Humanity in Christian Theology

The impact of grace on humanity in the NT and in the writings of Christian theologians throughout the two millennia of Christianity has evolved. St. Paul begins his magnum opus [his epistle to the Romans] in Romans 1:1-7 by reminding us that we receive grace and apostleship through Jesus to bring about the faithful obedience of the Gentiles. However, we could ask if the impact of grace [God's presence and love] described in St. Paul's epistles was described the same way throughout the two millennia of Christianity. My answer is: the Christian theology of grace evolved significantly throughout the two millennia of Christianity; therefore, we need to briefly examine the major shifts in the theology of grace. In my opinion, there have been at least six major shifts in Christianity's understanding of the impact of grace on humanity: <u>First</u>, grace in the NT; <u>Second</u>, St. Augustine's theology of grace; <u>Third</u>, St. Thomas Aquinas' theology of grace; <u>Fourth</u>, Martin Luther's theology of grace; <u>Fifth</u>, the Council of Trent's theology of grace; and <u>Sixth</u>, Karl Rahner SJ's, theology of grace. The key to understanding the evolution of the theology of grace is to understand the impact of God's grace on our human nature after each major shift in the theology of grace.

<u>First, the word grace is used explicitly throughout NT theology</u> beginning with St. Paul, who began to write approximately ten years after Jesus' death [ca. 45–63.] St. Paul described at least two specific impacts of God's grace on Christians: <u>First, grace seals us in Christ,</u> which is the initial step of knowing God's presence and love, in 2 Corinthians 1:21-22 "[21]But it is God who establishes us with you in Christ and has anointed us, [22]by putting his seal on us and giving us his Spirit in our hearts as a first installment." and <u>Second</u>, grace gives us the power to overcome our weaknesses. In his second extant epistle to the Corinthains, Paul told us that he was given a thorn to keep him humble. However, like most of us, Paul didn't want his thorn. So, Paul prayed to God to remove his thorn and he told us God's response to him in 2 Corinthians 12:8-9 "[8]Three times I appealed to the

Lord about this [his thorn], that it would leave me, [9]but he [God] said to me, '<u>My grace is sufficient for you, for power is made perfect in weakness.</u>'"

<u>Second, for St. Augustine's [354-430 CE], the impact of grace is moral.</u> God's grace restores our original nature, which was lost after the fall of Adam and Eve. The human will is compromised at birth [original sin] because of the sin of Adam and Eve, and it's subsequently compromised by our life choices. So, the impact of grace is to heal our will, which is wounded by sin and incapable of achieving the good that God designed it to achieve. For St. Augustine, grace is: "a new form of liberty through an internal modification of the human will... an inner working of God within freedom."[17] Bishop Augustine was involved in a debate with Bishop Pelagius [354–418 CE] about the degree to which we live in bondage to sin, because of the fall of Adam and Eve. Bishop Pelagius' theology emphasized human choice in salvation, which denied the impact of original sin. Bishop Pelagius located grace inside of human freedom, allowing us to use our God-given reason to choose between good and evil. Bishop Pelagius held that grace could be developed through a positive, loving, personal relationship with God, because it can be seen in Christ's teaching and example.

---

17   Roger Haight SJ, *The Experience and Language of Grace*, 36

However, Bishop Augustine did not share the optimism of Bishop Pelagius, because of his personal struggles with concupiscence. The Ecumenical Councils of Ephesus [431] and Orange [529] supported Bishop Augustine, which subsequently led to the Christian doctrine of original sin. The Councils of Ephesus and Orange may have agreed with St. Augustine because they were concerned that placing grace inside human freedom could lead humans to believe that they can save themselves, which Christian theology rejects. Bishop Augustine maintained the gratuitous nature of God's grace and he didn't let grace overpower our freedom; however, he was very willing to let sin overpower our freedom. In my opinion, the resolution of both Ecumenical Councils [Ephesus and Orange] on the interaction of grace and freedom was never completely resolved for some Christian believers, because even though we're oriented toward sin, we're also oriented toward God's offer of grace.

Third, for St. Thomas Aquinas [1225–1274], the impact of grace is ontological, because it makes us one with God. The Catholic Church directed St. Thomas to respond to the work of Aristotle, the naturalist, whose basic view was that human reason is sufficient to understand the world. This was the fundamental position of Bishop Pelagius and the position that was returned to by the Enlightenment Philosophers (e.g., Jean-Jacques Rousseau.) For Aquinas, sin wounds our human nature, but it does not destroy our nature or permanently overpower our freedom; so, grace is necessary to complete our human nature and create in us a new form. Grace is added to our nature because without grace, human nature is closed off from God.[18] For Aquinas, there are two kinds of grace: <u>first</u>, created grace caused by God's presence and love in our soul as its new form and <u>second</u>, uncreated grace, which is present in God before it becomes present in human beings through the Holy Spirit (e.g., through the sacraments of the Catholic Church.)

<u>Fourth, for Martin Luther [1483-1546], the impact of grace is God's forgiveness of our sins.</u> Human freedom is never free in relation to God. Our freedom begins in bondage because of original sin, and it stays in bondage because of our choices, which is essentially a return to St. Augustine's theology of grace. Humans remain powerless to change their utterly corrupt nature; so, we can only obtain righteousness because of Jesus' life, ministry, death, resurrection, and ascension. What God sees in us is Jesus' righteousness and not our own sinful human nature, which always remains sinful. So, only faith, only grace, and only scriptures can justify us before God. Although Luther was pessimistic about humanity's sinful nature, he was very optimistic about humanity's guaranteed salvation.

---

18 Roger Haight SJ, *The Experience and Language of Grace*, 123

Fifth, the Council of Trent [1545-1563] responded to Luther's theology of grace by telling us that the impact of grace is justification [righteousness], that is, we're pardoned, just as if we never sinned. The Council of Trent held that the impact of grace is to transform us in such a way that our nature is no longer intrinsically sinful, because we freely accept and cooperate with the infusion of God's grace in us through the work of the Holy Spirit. However, our justification can be lost through serious sin; so, our salvation is not guaranteed. Following from the epistle of James, the Council of Trent held that if you say you're faithful but your life doesn't demonstrate faithfulness, then you're not saved. Lutherans tend to say we're only saved by Christ, because we have no righteousness of our own, while Catholics say we're justified [made righteous] through the power of grace. In my opinion, today, Catholics and Lutherans both hold that we're saved by grace and having been saved we're called to do good works.

Sixth, for Karl Rahner SJ, the impact of grace is ontological, that is, grace builds on pure human nature. In Rahner's theology of grace, the impact of grace is to transform our capacity to love God, self, and others. Rahner essentially returned to Aquinas' ontological theology of grace, but he redefined Aquinas' theology by saying that pure human nature doesn't exist. If you took away God's grace, then you'd have pure human nature, but we live in a world permeated by the offer of God's grace [God's presence and love]; therefore, pure human nature is only a possibility, not a reality. Rahner's position is based on his belief in God's salvific will for humanity: "Our actual nature is never 'pure' nature. It is a nature installed in a supernatural order which man can never leave, even as a sinner and unbeliever. It is a nature, which is continually being determined (which does not mean justified) by the supernatural grace of salvation offered to it."[19] For Rahner, our nature is the way it is, because grace must be included. Most importantly, at the intersection of humanity and divinity, we obtain union with God through God's offer of grace, not through our pure human nature.

There are many corollaries to Rahner's theology of grace, but I'll just examine one, that is, how Rahner's theology of grace changes our understanding of how Catholic sacraments work.

<u>In the classic sacramental theology of grace</u>, the sacraments cause the grace that we receive (e.g., in the sacrament of the Eucharist we receive grace [God's presence and love] because we receive the transubstantiated body and blood of Christ.) In other words, grace touches the world at specific times to make grace available that was otherwise unavailable.

---

19 Karl Rahner SJ, <u>Theological Investigations</u> IV, "Nature and Grace," 183

In Rahner's theology of grace, the offer of grace permeates the world from the beginning of creation. Therefore, the sacraments do not create grace. Instead, they make the offer of grace [God's presence and love], which is already present everywhere, more accessible to us; therefore, grace causes the sacraments. For Catholics, sacraments and sacramentals (e.g., medals) make God's love present to us, but the offer of God's grace isn't limited to sacraments and sacramentals. Grace is available wherever a person realizes, in their freedom, that their existence is radically dependent on God.[20]

In my opinion, Rahner's theology of grace represents the current understanding of the theology of grace in the Catholic Church. Pope John XXIII [1881–1963] named Karl Rahner SJ, an official expert of the Second Vatican Council [1962–1965] and a member of the critically influential theological commission... For one conservative theologian, Rahner was regarded as the most powerful man at the Council.[21]

---

20 Karl Rahner SJ, Theological Investigations XIX, "On the Theology of Worship," 143

21 Ronald Modras, *Ignatian Humanism*, 232-233

CHAPTER FIVE

The Divine Theological Conditions that Make God's Offer of Grace Available to Humanity

Introduction

I've examined the human side of the intersection between humanity and divinity, that is, the theological conditions [existentials] that make us different from other beings, including God's many gifts to us, which are intended to lead us to a better righteousness. I've examined the actual intersection of humanity and divinity, God's offer of grace [God's presence and love], through what Rahner calls "the supernatural existential [condition]" through which God grasps us, because we're spirits in the world designed to hear God's Word. In addition, I examined the impact of the Christian theology grace on humanity through six major shifts in the Christian understanding of the theology of grace.

Next, I examine the divine side of the intersection between humanity and divinity, where we find the Trinity of God's presence and love operating in our everyday lives through grace [God's presence and love] in three distinct ways: <u>First</u>, God the Father's love is present to us (e.g., throughout God's creation and throughout the scriptures); <u>Second</u>, the Holy Spirit's love is present to us (e.g., externally in the universe and/or internally in our hearts and minds); and <u>Third</u>, God's love is present in the historical Jesus of Nazareth. Whether we experience God's presence and love through our everyday unthematic transcendent experience of God or through our thematic experiences of God (e.g., praying, reading and studying God's scriptures), all of our experiences trace back to a single source, which Judeo-Christian believers call YHWH or God.

God's Love Is Present throughout God's Creation

We begin our search for God the Father's presence and love in God's theocentric creation, which was permeated with the offer of grace from the beginning of creation. Roger Haight SJ described God's presence and love as the within of God's creation: "God is within this world, and symbols make God present. By creation, incarnation, and grace God becomes the very within of things… The world itself is mystery because God is found at its core... The creator is the within of all things, their reason for being, their intelligibility, their order, their logic. God's will is written into being itself."[22]

In the English language, the word love has several different meanings. However, in the Greek language, there are different words for the different kinds of love (e.g., eros [passionate love], philia [brotherly love], and agape [an unconditional self-sacrificing divine love.]) God's divine love for humanity is a supernatural agape love that faithfully and steadfastly continues despite humanity's disobedience and rebellion against God's guidance for us. God's agape love forgives again and again and again.

In my opinion, no one teaches us about God [for Christian believers, God the Father.] We experience a rudimentary understanding of God's presence and love in the world and in our being before we're ever taught about God the Father. We can see God throughout God's creation by observing the mysteries of nature and the mysteries of the animal kingdom. I will briefly examine two psalms that help us to find God's presence and love in our everyday lives: <u>First</u>, the opening verses of Psalm 19, which describe God's presence and love designed <u>into God's creation</u> and <u>Second</u>, the opening verses of Psalm 139, which describe God's presence and love designed <u>into our humanity</u>.

---

22 Roger Haight SJ, *Dynamics of Theology*, 157

Psalm 19 – God's Presence, Love, and Self-Communication in God's Creation

In the opening verses of Psalm 19, the psalmist describes God's presence, love, and self-communication to us by personifying and animating various parts of nature, because we can see and know God through God's works without having to rely on abstract metaphysical speculations about God. Psalm 19:1-6 resonates with many psalms that describe the majesty of God the Father (e.g., Psalms 8; 24:1ff; 33:6ff; 65:5ff; 95:4ff; 102:25-28; 104; 135:5-7; 136:5ff; 146:6ff.) The psalmist begins his description of God's presence and love in creation in Psalm 19:1-4a "[1]The heavens [the sun, moon, stars, planets] are telling the glory of God; and the firmament [the sky] proclaims his handiwork. [2]Day to day pours forth speech, and night to night declares knowledge. [3]There is no speech, nor are there words; their voice is not heard; [4a]yet their voice goes out through all the earth, and their words to the end of the world." The psalmist is certain that God's presence and love for us is visible to everyone through nature's wonders, which witness to the majesty and glory of God, because a master is known by their work. The heavens continually reveal God's secrets to us; which resonates with Psalm 97:6 "[6]The heavens proclaim his [God's] righteousness; and all the peoples behold his glory." The heavens speak in God's language, a language that transcends human languages, and a language that reveals God's presence and love to everyone.

Matthew's Gospel provides an analogy to the psalmist's observations, in Matthew 7:16 "[16]You will know them by their fruits." Matthew 7:16 resonates with many verses of scripture (e.g., Matthew 7:20; Luke 6:43-45; Colossians 1:9-10; Psalm 92:12-15; Jeremiah 17:7-8.) God's fruits include the wonders of nature (e.g., the sun brings life to all things on earth as the course of the sun covers the earth in Psalm 19:4b-6.) So, the sun, which enables the beauty of all things in Isaiah 45:5-6; Psalms 113:3-4; 50:1; and Malachi 1:11, is a fruit of God's work and a manifestation of God's presence, love, and self-communication to everyone.

Psalm 139 – God's Presence in Our Lives

In the opening verses of Psalm 139, the psalmist is terrified of God's presence in every part of his life, because the psalmist is initially thinking of God as a modern-day Orwellian Big Brother. So, he struggles in several ways to escape from God's presence and love. In the opening verses of the psalm, the psalmist acknowledges that God knows everything about him and that scares him, in Psalm 139:1-5 "¹O LORD, you have searched me and known me. ²You know when I sit down and when I rise up; you discern my thoughts from far away. ³You search out my path and my lying down, and are acquainted with all my ways. ⁴Even before a word is on my tongue, O LORD, you know it completely. ⁵You hem me in, behind and before, and lay your hand upon me."

The psalmist's initial reaction to God's presence and love is fear, which causes him to try and escape from God in Psalm 139:7-12. The psalmist explores various ways to escape from God's presence and love through a series of hypothetical statements (e.g., Psalm 139:8 "⁸If I ascend to heaven, you are there; if I make my bed in Sheol, you are there.") As a final escape plan, the psalmist imagines a magical dark place where he can hide from God's presence and love in Psalm 139:11-12 "¹¹If I say, "Surely the darkness shall cover me, and the light around me become night," ¹²even the darkness is not dark to you; the night is as bright as the day, for darkness is as light to you." Eventually, the psalmist realizes that he is unable to escape from God's presence and love even in his imaginary magical dark place, because God's presence and love would light it up, which resonates with John 1:5 "⁵The light [truth] shines in the darkness, and the darkness did not overcome it." The psalmist's experience also resonates with the prophet Jonah, who discovered the hard way that he could not escape from God's presence and love (cf. Jonah 1–2.)

In the next part of Psalm 139:13-16 the psalmist begins to understand that God's presence and love is actually a blessing in his life, even though he cannot fully understand the Absolute Mystery of God. The psalmist finally praises God for creating him, in Psalm 139:14 "¹⁴I praise you, for I am fearfully and wonderfully made. Wonderful are your works; that I know very well."

God is continually trying to guide our lives in order to help us become the persons we're intended to become, a self-for-others. Therefore, we need to find the same clarity that the psalmist and Jonah eventually found; that is, we cannot escape from God's presence and love. Instead, we need to follow the counsel of the apostle Peter, who told us what we really need to escape from in 2 Peter 1:3-4 "³His [Jesus'] divine power has given us everything needed for life and godliness, through the knowledge of him who called us by his own glory and goodness. ⁴Thus he has given us, through these things, his precious and very great promises, so that through them you may <u>escape from the corruption that is in the world</u> because of lust, and may become participants of the divine nature." The faithful God of steadfast love is always and everywhere present to us. We need to be open to the experience of God's presence and love in our lives.

God's Love Is Present through God's Holy Spirit

Introduction

For Jewish believers, God's presence and love is recorded in human history throughout the OT. For Catholic believers, the Nicene creed acknowledges that God has spoken through the prophets. The scriptures assure us that God's Holy Spirit has been active from the beginning of God's creation process in Genesis 1:1-2. In my opinion, we can find God's presence and love through the impact of God's Holy Spirit in two ways: <u>First</u>, <u>externally</u> throughout God's creation and throughout God's scriptures and <u>Second</u>, for Christian believers, <u>internally</u> through Jesus' gift to us of an Advocate, who continues to teach us Jesus' revelations about His Father, in John 14:26 "[26]But the Advocate, <u>the Holy Spirit</u>, whom the Father will send in my name, will teach you everything, and remind you of all that I have said to you."

<u>Finding God's Holy Spirit in our lives</u>

<u>We can find the Holy Spirit externally in our lives</u>, because the Holy Spirit intervened in human affairs throughout OT and NT narratives. I will briefly examine six scriptural examples of God's Holy Spirit active in God's creation: <u>First</u>, we can find God's Holy Spirit externally intervening in the first Genesis creation story in Genesis 1:1-2 "[1]In the beginning when

God created the heavens and the earth, ²the earth was a formless void and darkness covered the face of the deep, while <u>a wind from God [the Spirit of God]</u> swept over the face of the waters"; <u>Second</u>, we can find God's Holy Spirit externally intervening to save God's chosen people throughout Israel's history (e.g., in the miracles described in the Exodus narrative); <u>Third</u>, we can find God's Holy Spirit externally intervening in the mysterious deaths of one hundred and eighty-five thousand Assyrian soldiers, who were preparing to destroy the Southern Kingdom of Judah in Isaiah 37:36; 2 Kings 19:35; <u>Fourth</u>, we can find God's Holy Spirit externally present during Jesus' baptism in the form of a dove in all four Gospels, in Mark 1:10; Matthew 3:16; Luke 3:22; John 1:32; <u>Fifth</u>, we can find God's Holy Spirit externally intervening in Luke's Gospel, when the angel Gabriel appeared to Mary and explained that she would conceive a child by the Holy Spirit in Luke 1:35; and <u>Sixth</u>, we can find God's Holy Spirit externally present in Simeon in Luke's Gospel in Luke 2:25 "²⁵Now there was a man in Jerusalem whose name was Simeon; this man was righteous and devout, looking forward to the consolation of Israel, and <u>the Holy Spirit rested on him</u>."

We can find the Holy Spirit internally in our lives. For Jewish believers, the need for the internal presence of God's Holy Spirit was prophesied by all three of Israel's major prophets, in Jeremiah 31:31-34; Ezekiel 11:19-20; 36:26-27, and Isaiah 63:11-13, because Jeremiah, Ezekiel, and Isaiah realized that something had to change theologically in order to make God's love more present to the people of God and through them to the nations. I want to briefly examine one of the prophetic descriptions of the shift that was prophesied in OT theology, in Jeremiah 31:31-33 "³¹The days are surely coming, says the LORD, when <u>I will make a new covenant with the house of Israel and the house of Judah</u>. ³²It will not be like the covenant that I made with their ancestors when I took them by the hand to bring them out of the land of Egypt—a covenant that they broke, though I was their husband, says the LORD. ³³But this is the covenant that I will make with the house of Israel after those days, says the LORD: <u>I will put my law within them, and I will write it on their hearts</u>; and I will be their God, and they shall be my people." Jeremiah, Ezekiel, and Isaiah understood the need for a new covenant between God and Israel. This covenant must include God's commandments being written on the hearts of the Israelites, because writing commandments on tablets and scrolls proved to be insufficient. In my opinion, Jeremiah was teaching Jewish believers that they need to move beyond the idea of guaranteed admission into the kingdom [reign] of God; they need to understand and accept a new covenant with God written on their hearts. The impact of this new covenant is described in Jeremiah 32:36-44, as a supernatural gift from God to His covenant people.[23]

We can find the Holy Spirit internally in our lives. In my opinion, Jesus' indwelling advocate [God's Holy Spirit] is the actualization of the prophesies of Jeremiah, Ezekiel, and Isaiah. God's indwelling Holy Spirit is a practical helper, who helps Christian believers in at least seven ways: <u>First</u>, God's Holy Spirit guides us to God's truth in John 14:16-17 "¹⁶And I will ask the Father, and he will give you another Advocate, to be with you forever. ¹⁷This is the Spirit of truth, whom the world cannot receive, because it neither sees him nor knows him. You know him, because he abides with you, and he will be in you;" <u>Second,</u> God's Holy Spirit continually reminds us through the sacrament of Holy Eucharist that Jesus is the mediator of a new covenant, in Luke 22:19-20 "¹⁹Then he took a loaf of bread, and when he had given thanks, he broke it and gave it to them, saying, 'This is my body, which is given for you. Do this in remembrance of me.' ²⁰And he did the same with the cup after supper, saying, '"This cup that is poured out for you is the new covenant in my blood"; <u>Third,</u> God's Holy Spirit helps us to pray to God, in Romans 8:26-27 "²⁶Likewise the Spirit helps us in our weakness;

---

23 Leslie C. Allen, *Jeremiah*, 357

for we do not know how to pray as we ought, but that very Spirit intercedes with sighs too deep for words. [27]And God, who searches the heart, knows what is the mind of the Spirit, because the Spirit intercedes for the saints [believers] according to the will of God"; <u>Fourth</u>, through the intercession of God's Holy Spirit we are led to our inheritance, in Romans 8:14-17 "[14]For all who are led by the Spirit of God are children of God. [15]For you did not receive a spirit of slavery to fall back into fear, but you have received a spirit of adoption. When we cry, 'Abba! Father!' [16]it is that very Spirit bearing witness with our spirit that we are children of God, [17]and <u>if children, then heirs</u>, heirs of God and joint heirs with Christ—if, in fact, we suffer with him so that we may also be glorified with him." Our inheritance includes God's eternal promises (e.g., Hebrews 13:5 "I will never leave you or forsake you."); <u>Fifth</u>, the indwelling of God's Holy Spirit orients us toward God's offer of grace. St. Paul summoned Christians to live by the Spirit of God in Galatians 5:16-26, because God knows what we need. God's Holy Spirit helps us to understand Jesus' revelations to us in the scriptures (e.g., John 16:7-11); <u>Sixth</u>, with St. Paul, Christian believers can find the help they need through God's indwelling Holy Spirit, in Romans 8:11 "[11]If the Spirit of him who raised Jesus from the dead dwells in you, he who raised Christ from the dead will give life to your mortal bodies also through his Spirit that dwells in you."; and Seventh, God's Holy Spirit helps us to conform to the will of God, which leads us to a better righteousness, in Romans 8:13 "[13]for if you live according to the flesh, you will die; but if by the Spirit you put to death the deeds of the body, you will live."

God's Love Is Present through the Ministry of the Historical Jesus of Nazareth

Introduction

For Christian believers, the historical Jesus of Nazareth is the centerpiece of NT scripture narratives, because we believe that Jesus is the fullest revelation of God's presence and love, in John 1:1-5, 14; Matthew 1:23; Luke 1:35; Mark 1:1; and Galatians 4:4-7. In the first creation story in my book, humanity was created, in Genesis 1:26a "²⁶Then God said, 'Let us make humankind in our image according to our likeness.'" For Christian believers, Jesus is the image of God, in 2 Corinthians 4:4 "⁴In their case the god of this world has blinded the minds of the unbelievers, to keep them from seeing the light of the gospel of <u>the glory of Christ, who is the image of God</u>." Jesus is also the likeness of God, described in Ephesians 4:24 "²⁴clothe yourselves with the new self, created according to the likeness of God in true righteousness and holiness." Humanity was created and designed to love God and depend on God to love and sustain us. We need to become righteous and holy, and we need to return to our original design in Wisdom 2:23.

In my opinion, no one teaches us about God the Father and St. Paul confirms that in Romans 1:19-23. However, we do need to be taught about Jesus, the Son of God. For Christian believers, Jesus is God, in John 10:30 "³⁰The Father and I are one." Why do we need to turn to Jesus to find the fullest revelation of God's presence and love? The answer is found in John 1:18 "No one has ever seen God. It is God the only Son, who is close to the Father's heart, <u>who has made him known</u>." The four canonical Gospels provide the easiest way to learn about Jesus, who assures us that we can know God the Father by knowing Him, in John 14:7a "⁷If you know me, you will know my Father also." It is through the revelations of the historical person, Jesus the Christ, who is "full of grace [God's presence and love] and truth" in John 1:14, that we can begin to understand the transcendent Absolute Mystery of God the Father, because an encounter with Jesus is an encounter with God's presence and love.

There are a myriad of books written on every aspect of Jesus' life and ministry. In this part of my book, I want to briefly examine five aspects of the historical Jesus' life and ministry: <u>First</u>, the historical world that Jesus was born into; <u>Second</u>, Jesus' two audiences; <u>Third</u>, finding God's presence and love in Jesus' ministry; <u>Fourth</u>, finding a better righteousness; and <u>Fifth</u>, finding the Judeo-Christian hope of the kingdom [reign] of God.

First, Jesus' World

<u>The historical world that Jesus was born into</u> lived under Roman domination. However, we begin to

study the historical Jesus by understanding at least three conditions that preceded and influenced Jesus' ministry before it ever began: the social political remnants of the Maccabean revolt; Israel's prophetic literature transmuted into apocalyptic literature; and Jesus' probable upbringing in the Jewish world into which He was born.

The social political remnants of the Maccabean revolt were escalated because of a civil war in Israel between the Pharisees and Sadducees, which was ended by the Roman general Pompey, who helped the Pharisees defeat the Sadducees in Jerusalem. Subsequently, Israel became part of the Roman Empire. However, before the Romans took control, Israel's social and political factions were previously defined by the Maccabean Revolt [ca. 167-160 BCE.] The Israelites, led by the Maccabees, rebelled against the Seleucid Empire and against Hellenistic influence on Jewish life and the Jewish temple. The resulting social/political society that Jesus was born into consisted of four major polarized factions: the Sadducees, the Pharisees, the Zealots, and the Essenes. These four factions became even more entrenched in their belief systems under Roman domination: "As taxation increasingly oppressed ordinary people, and as famine and drought reduced substantial portions of the population to poverty, the wealthy – including many members of the high priestly families, the Sadducees, were filling their own coffers. Meanwhile farmers, forced to sell their land at reduced prices, found themselves reduced to tenant laborers often working for absentee landlords... Between the laborers and landowners came a social stratum of artisans and traders. Neither impoverished nor financially secure... It was perhaps from this group that the Pharisees and the followers of Jesus both gained adherents, and from this group as well may have come the Zealots of the revolt against Rome in 66-70 CE... The Qumran community [the Essenes], John the Baptist, and several charismatic leaders in one way or another addressed the spiritual and material needs of the population, by variously promising revolt against Rome, the deity's direct intervention in human affairs, or the assurance of life after death."[24] These four social-political factions were deeply embedded in the Israel that Jesus was born into.

Israel's prophetic literature transmuted into apocalyptic literature after the last prophet, Malachi, ended prophetic history. The book of Malachi is dated in the Persian period [ca. 539 BCE–325 BCE.] However, apocalyptic literature dominated theological society during Jesus' ministry; it was in the air. Dan Harrington SJ, wrote a wonderful book called, *The Maccabean Revolt*,

---

24 Coogan, Ed., Jo Ann Hackett, "*The Oxford History of the Biblical* World, "Visions of Kingdoms," 482

which describes how deeply apocalyptic literature dominated the world that Jesus was born into and its subsequent impact on Christianity. "Jesus' prayer <u>'thy kingdom come'</u> expresses the longing of Jews and Christians for the coming of God's kingdom as in Daniel and other apocalyptic writings… Apocalypticism provided many of the theological terms and concepts for Jesus and the early Christians – so much so that apocalyptic has been called the "<u>mother of Christian theology</u>…" Resurrection was originally part of the complex of beliefs that make up Jewish apocalypticism. In fact, the resurrection of the dead is one element in the Jewish scenario of events that are to accompany the full coming of God's kingdom [reign."][25] Even though Israel lived under Roman domination, Israel's theological, social, and political circumstances were predefined by its history.

<u>Jesus' upbringing in the Jewish world into which he was born</u> is documented by John Meier: "Jesus of Nazareth was born – most likely in Nazareth, not Bethlehem – ca 7 or 6 BCE, a few years before the death of King Herod the Great (4 BCE.) After an unexceptional upbringing in a pious family of Jewish peasants in Lower Galilee, he was attracted to the movement of John the Baptist, who began his ministry in the region of the Jordan Valley around the end of 27 CE or the

---

25 Dan Harrington SJ, *The Maccabean Revolt*, 129

beginning of 28 CE. Baptized by John, Jesus soon struck out on his own, beginning his public ministry early in 28, when he was around thirty-three or thirty-four years old."[26] For Christian believers, Jesus was born and raised a pious Jewish boy, who understood Judaism from His upbringing but always with two different perspectives, because hundreds of years after Jesus' death, the Council of Chalcedon [451], declared that Jesus was fully human and fully divine.

Second, Jesus' Two Audiences

<u>Jesus first audience was primarily Jewish believers</u>, who lived in and around Israel in a very poor agrarian society. Jesus' parables [stories] were often agricultural (e.g., the Parable of the Sower), because agricultural stories resonated with Jesus' primary audience. Today, people might have difficulty understanding what Jesus said (e.g., His agricultural metaphors) but the Jewish people to whom Jesus was ministering and the Jewish leadership, who were watching Jesus' miracles and listening to Jesus' teaching, understood exactly what Jesus was saying and doing. Jesus' ministry clashed with the Jewish religious establishment of His day in several ways (e.g., Jesus offered a new covenant outside of proper channels, in 1 Corinthians 11:25; Luke 22:20;

---

[26] John P. Meier, *A Marginal Jew: Rethinking the Historical Jesus*, Volume One, 407

Hebrews 8:8; 9:15; 12:24; Jesus forgave sins by His own authority in Mark. 2:10; Matthew 9:16; Luke 5:24; Jesus offered salvation by His own authority in Luke 19:1-10; Jesus attacked the symbols of Judaism (e.g., using the temple as a marketplace;) and Jesus invited <u>everyone</u> to repent and become part of the kingdom [reign] of God including the poor and sinners.)[27]

In modern-day American consciousness, we would have a problem if someone claimed to be the Son of God and claimed to forgive sins. How did Jewish believers understand a man, who claimed be the Messiah, the Son of God, and who claimed to forgive sins? In Matthew's and Luke's Gospels, after John the Baptist was arrested and imprisoned, John sent his disciples to ask Jesus a question in Matthew 11:2-3 "²When John heard in prison what the Messiah was doing, he sent word by his disciples ³and said to him, 'Are you the one who is to come, or are we to wait for another?'" Their question was are You the Messiah or should we keep waiting? In my opinion, the question from the disciples of John the Baptist describes the Jewish consciousness of Jesus' day, that is, Jewish believers were waiting for the long-awaited Messiah (e.g., King David redivivus, not Isaiah's suffering servant.) For Christian believers, God remains transcendent but through Jesus no

---

27 Wright, *Jesus and the Victory of God*, 274

longer distant, because an encounter with Jesus is an encounter with God's presence and love.

How did Jewish leadership understand Jesus? Jesus was not arrested, tried, and murdered because people were confused about His teaching. Jesus was arrested, tried, and murdered, because the Jewish/Roman leadership would not permit Jesus' teaching to gather further support from Jewish believers and/or the Gentile believers. After Jesus' death, His first, primarily Jewish audience tenuously became a separate sect within Judaism until the second temple was destroyed and the Israelites experienced their second Diaspora [ca. 70.] At that point in history, Judaism and Christianity necessarily became separate religions.

<u>Jesus' second audience was primarily Gentile believers, who lived in a predominantly pagan world outside of Israel.</u> Jesus' second audience were generally unfamiliar with Jewish theology, so St. Paul and other Christian missionaries explained both the teaching of Jesus and the teaching of Jewish theology to Gentile Christian believers as necessary (e.g., Christian missionaries were teaching Gentiles about the significance of monotheism.) Despite the challenges, St. Paul and other Christian missionaries recruited Gentile believers, who eventually became the dominant constituency in Christianity. Hundreds of years after Jesus' death, the Gentile/Jewish believers in Christianity

became the official religion of the Roman Empire beginning with the Roman Emperor Constantine the Great [after the Council of Nicaea [ca. 325]] and finalized under the Roman Emperor Theodosius [ca. 380.] Christian believers came to understand the salvific significance of Jesus, the Christ [the Messiah], who is our Lord and Savior, and they came to understand that the actualization of OT promises and prophecies were fulfilled by Jesus in the fullness of time. The leitmotif in Matthew's Gospel is: Jesus is the fulfillment of OT prophecies, which resonates with Galatians 4:4-5 and Ephesians 1:3-14.

For Christian believers, God [Jesus] became incarnate [human] for many reasons, including: <u>First</u>, to correct the blindness that had again fallen on humanity, in 2 Corinthains 4; <u>Second</u>, to more fully reveal His Father to humanity, because Jesus is the visible image of the invisible God, in John 1:1-2, 14 and Colossians 1:15-20; <u>Third</u>, to provide us with an additional access point to the Absolute Mystery of God; and <u>Fourth</u>, to become the actualization of Second Isaiah's suffering servant songs in Isaiah 42:1-4; 49:1-6; 50:4-9; 52:13–53:12, which means to become a sacrificial atonement for the sins of humanity.

Third, Finding God's Presence and Love Through Jesus' Ministry

Jesus' ministry, death, resurrection, and ascension back to His Father describe the kind of Son that Jesus is. For Christian believers, Jesus' revelations about His Father actually answer some of our questions (e.g., Jesus taught us in John 14:7 "⁷<u>If you know me, you will know my Father also</u>. From now on you do know him and have seen him.") This is a call to everyone to read and study the historical Jesus, the Son of God, by studying the Gospels. We can find God's presence and love in our lives when we understand and believe who Jesus is, in John 8:12; 9:5 "I am the light [truth] of the world." When we surrender our lives to God in faith, trust, hope, and love, Jesus lights our way out of darkness, out of temptation, out of the trials and burdens that we sometimes don't understand (e.g., physical difficulties, financial difficulties, relationship difficulties.) We can find God's presence and love throughout Jesus' ministry, because Jesus is the only Son of God and an encounter with Jesus is an encounter with God's presence and love.

Isaiah taught us that there is a difference between our thoughts and God's thoughts in Isaiah 55:8-9 "⁸For my thoughts are not your thoughts, nor are your ways my ways, says the Lord. ⁹For as the heavens are higher than the earth, so are my ways higher than your ways and my thoughts than your thoughts." But what if were possible to know God's thoughts? Words matter, and Jesus taught us where His words come from in John 7:16-17 "[16]Then Jesus answered them, 'My teaching is not mine but his who sent me. [17]Anyone who resolves to do the will of God will know whether the teaching is from God or whether I am speaking on my own.'" In other words, we can know what God is thinking by carefully reading Jesus' words and revelations recorded in the four Gospels.

Jesus' ministry had many components (e.g., bridging the chasm between humanity and divinity in Luke 16:26; John 14:6, revealing His Father, teaching, performing miracles, and fulfilling Isaiah's suffering servant's role by dying for our sins.) During His ministry, Jesus taught us how to be in relationship with His Father (e.g., how to pray to His Father in Mathew 6:7-15; Mark 11:25-26; Luke11:1-4.) Jesus taught us in parables (e.g., the Parable of the Sower in Matthew 13:1-9; Mark 4:1-9; Luke 8:4-8.) Jesus healed people (e.g., Matthew 8:1-4.) Jesus performed miracles (e.g., John 2:1-10.) Jesus performed exorcisms (e.g., Matthew 8:14-16; Mark 1:32-34; Luke 4:40-41.) And Jesus resuscitated people (e.g., Matthew 9:18-26; Mark 5:21-42; Luke 8:40-56; John 11:17-44.)

There are countless books written on all the aspects of Jesus' ministry but I want to focus on one aspect of

Jesus' ministry, that is, His teaching in "The Sermon on the Mount" discourse in Matthew's Gospel in Matthew 5–7, because I believe that "The Sermon on the Mount" discourse provides the most comprehensive ethical teaching in literature. Jesus' Sermon on the Mount teaches us how to find a better righteousness: through nine beatitudes in Matthew 5:3-16; through six antithesis, which help us to build a hedge around the OT law in Matthew 5:17-48[28]; through correctly performing three acts of piety in Mathew 6:1-18; and through Jesus' teachings on correct Chistian social and economic practices in Matthew 6:19–7:12. However, I cannot go into detail on the entire Sermon on the Mount, so I want to focus on what I consider to be the pivotal verse in the Sermon of the Mount, Matthew 6:33, because in this verse Jesus tells us what's most important to Him and therefore what should be most important to us. Matthew 6:33 "[3]But <u>strive first</u> [what's important] <u>for the kingdom [reign] of God</u> and <u>his righteousness</u>, and <u>all these things</u> [everything we need] <u>will be given to you as well</u>."

Jesus used the phrase the kingdom [reign] of God because it crystalized the hopes and expectations of the Jewish believers.[29] A quick study of Matthew 6:33 reveals Jesus' guidance to all Christians. Jesus specifically told

---

28 Frank J. Matera, *NT Christology*, 45

29 Zachary Hayes, *Visions of a Future*, 44

us to "Strive first" for the kingdom [reign] of God and his righteousness. I'm going to first describe our need to strive for a better righteousness and then I'll describe our need to strive for the kingdom [reign] of God. In the final phrase of Matthew 6:33, Jesus assured us that if we strive first [if we focus on what's important], then all our everyday needs will be satisfied, in Matthew 6:25-34.

Fourth, Finding a Better Righteousness

In my opinion, the entire Sermon on the Mount describes Jesus' teaching on how to find a better righteousness. For John Reumann, in Matthew 6:33, "God's righteousness" is plainly parallel to "God's kingdom." As the beatitudes show, the kingdom (cf. Matthew 5:3,10) is God's future eschatological gift. So also is righteousness (cf. Matthew 5:6.) In that the kingdom is both present and future in Matthew, so also is righteousness."[30]

The simplest definition of human righteousness is conforming to the will of God. The primary benefit of striving for a better righteousness is to live a more fulfilling and abundant life by living in a positive, loving relationship with God. In St. Paul's letter to the Ephesians, we're told that we need to clothe ourselves

---

[30] John Reumann, *Righteousness in the New Testament*, 131

in righteousness and holiness in order to live in God's presence and love, in Ephesians 4:22-24 "²²You were taught to put away your former way of life, your old self, corrupt and deluded by its lusts, ²³and to be renewed in the spirit of your minds, ²⁴and to <u>clothe yourselves with the new self, created according to the likeness of God in true righteousness and holiness</u>."

One way to achieve a better righteousness is to examine God's righteousness in the OT (e.g., God's steadfast love for His chosen people, God's faithfulness to His promises to Israel, God's faithfulness to His covenants with Israel, and God's faithfulness through the prophets that God sent to guide the Israelites.) For John Reumann, "There is absolutely no concept in the Old Testament with so central a significance for all the relationships of human life as that of <u>shah</u> [righteousness.] It is the standard not only for man's relationship to God, but also for his relationships to his fellows, reaching right down to ... the animals and to his natural environment ... it embraces the whole of Israelite life."[31] God's faithfulness and righteousness were revealed to us in order to bring about our own faithfulness and righteousness, in Romans 3:21-31, because God demands faithfulness and righteousness from us.

---

31 Reumann, *Righteousness in the New Testament*, 12

Jesus specifically told us that we need to find a better righteousness than Israel's religious leaders, in Matthew 5:20 "²⁰For I tell you, unless your righteousness exceeds that of the scribes and Pharisees, you will never enter the kingdom [reign] of heaven [God]." St. Paul followed Jesus' instructions and taught Christian believers how do find a better righteousness. St. Paul pointed to God's covenant with Abraham before the Law existed, in Romans 4:9b-10 "⁹ᵇWe say, 'Faith was reckoned to Abraham as righteousness.' ¹⁰How then was it reckoned to him? Was it before or after he had been circumcised? It was not after, but before he was circumcised." St. Paul then applied God's promise of Abraham's righteousness in Genesis 12:7a; 15:5-6; 1 Maccabees 2:52; Sirach 44:19-21 to Christians, because Christian belief in Jesus is analogous to Abraham's belief in God in Romans 4:22-25 "²²Therefore his [Abraham's] faith 'was reckoned [credited] to him as righteousness.' ²³Now the words, 'it was reckoned to him,' were written not for his sake alone, ²⁴but for ours also. It [righteousness] will be reckoned to us who believe in him who raised Jesus our Lord from the dead, who was handed over to death for our trespasses and who was raised for our justification." St. Paul's underlying point is that we cannot find righteousness by following the Law, because we cannot faithfully follow the Law (e.g., we cannot consistently keep the Ten Commandments.) For Christian believers, we can only find a better righteousness through faith in Jesus.

We receive God's gift of righteousness in the same way that we receive God's gift of grace [God's presence and love], that is, we receive an unmerited gift from God through our faith in Jesus. This is affirmed in Habakkuk 2:4 "⁴Look at the proud! Their spirit is not right in them, but <u>the righteous live by their faith</u>." John Bright assured us that righteousness is not rule keeping; rather, it requires total dedication to the will of the Father, which can be summed up in the word "love."[32] In addition, St. Paul assured us that the only path to true freedom is following God, in Romans 6:16 "¹⁶Do you not know that if you present yourselves to anyone as obedient slaves, you are slaves of the one whom you obey, either of sin, which leads to death, or of obedience, which leads to righteousness?" We need to strive first for God's righteousness, because in Matthew 6:33, Jesus taught us that it should be one of the two most important pursuits in our lives.

Fifth, Finding the Judeo-Christian Hope of the Kingdom [Reign] of God

In Matthew 6:33, Jesus taught us that finding the kingdom [reign] of God should be the other most

---

32 Bright, *The Kingdom of God*, 205

important pursuit in our lives. And Jesus taught us that we need to focus on finding imperishable heavenly treasures rather than being anxious about the necessities of life, because they only distract us from God's presence and love, in Matthew 6:19-21 and Luke 12:16-21. However, the kingdom [reign] of God remains a somewhat nebulous term (e.g., for Dan Harrington, "it is impossible to define something whose fullness is transcendent (it is God's kingdom) and future (it is God's to bring on "the day of the Lord."")[33] Nevertheless, John P. Meier tells us that the phrase "kingdom of God" appears throughout the NT: in Mark (13 times), Q (13 times), Matthew (25 times), Luke (6 times), and John (2 times), in Paul's undisputed letters in 1 Thessalonians 2:12; Galatians 5:21; 1 Corinthains 4:20; 6:9-10 [twice]; 15:24, 50; Romans 14:17, and in Paul's disputed letters in 2 Thessalonians 1:5; Colossians 1:13; 4:11; Ephesians 5:5; 2 Timothy 4:1, 18.[34]

I want to briefly examine four aspects of the kingdom [reign] of God: <u>First</u>, the origin of Jesus' phrase the kingdom [reign] of God; <u>Second</u>, Jesus' understanding of the kingdom [reign] of God; <u>Third</u>, who is invited into the kingdom [reign] of God; and <u>Fourth</u>, what condition must occur to permanently bring about the kingdom [reign] of God?

---

33   Harrington, *Who is Jesus?* 23

34   John P. Meier, *A Marginal Jew-Volume-Two*, 238

First, the origin of the phrase the kingdom [reign] of God

For John Bright, the kingdom [reign] of God provides a unifying theme throughout the Old Testament and the New Testament. There are many references to God's kingdom [reign] in the OT (e.g., 1 Chronicles 17:14; 28:5; 29:11; Psalms. 103:19; 145:13; 47, 93; 96; 97; 98; 99; Daniel 2:44; 4:3; 4:34; 7:27,) in the Synoptic Gospels, and in the Apocrypha in Wisdom 10:10; 6:4, 17-20; Sirach 36:1-17.) For Bright, the beginning of the theme "the kingdom [reign] of God" is most clearly understood in the Sinai covenant, because the people of Israel as a whole began to live under the rule of their God. Israel entered Canaan as a monotheistic people in a pagan world intent on following God's Covenant Law: "The notion of a people of God, called to live under the rule of God, begins just here, and with it the notion of the Kingdom of God."[35]

For John Bright, the OT provides the background story behind Jesus' phrase "the kingdom [reign] of God," because the nation of Israel began as a federation of twelve tribes united by their belief in YHWH's rule. King David and King Solomon gave power, prestige, and treasure to Israel; however, after King Solomon died, Israel suffered a schism, because the ten Northern tribes realized that excessive taxation and tolerated paganism were not signs from God. The

---

35 Bright, *The Kingdom of God*, 28

Southern Kingdom of Judah produced a few good kings (e.g., Hezekiah, Josiah) but the kings in the Northern Kingdom of Israel were all considered poor imitations of King David, which created the need for the Israelites to somehow return to the rule of God. It's through these circumstances that the of the metaphor of the kingdom [reign] of God emerged publicly, because the kingdom-metaphor renewed the hopes and aspirations of Jewish believers.

Second, Jesus' Understanding of the Kingdom [Reign] of God

Jesus was ministering to Jewish believers, whose expectations and hopes came from prophetic literature, apocalyptic literature, and what the rabbis had spoken to Jewish believers for centuries (e.g., God will eventually establish His Kingdom.)[36] Despite the hopes and expectations of the Israelites during Jesus' ministry, even when Jesus showed His apostles who He is in His transfiguration, they still didn't get it, in Mark 9:2-8. It was only after Jesus' death, resurrection, and ascension back to His Father that His apostles and disciples finally understood that Jesus is Son of God, in Mark 15:39.

In my opinion, Jesus emphasized the phrase kingdom [reign] of God in order to be a credible first century Jewish prophet to His first [Jewish] audience. The horizon and content of Jesus' teaching in the Synoptic Gospels is symbolized by Jesus' phrase the kingdom [reign] of God (e.g., Mark 1:15.) Jesus wasn't trying to teach His first, primarily Jewish, audience about an unknown God; He was trying to correct their misunderstanding of His Father and the kingdom [reign] of His Father, which was different from their hopes and expectations. Jesus described the importance

---

[36] Morna Hooker, *The Gospel According to Saint Mark*, 55

of the kingdom [reign] of God to His disciples and us (e.g., He taught His disciples and us that John the Baptist is greater than any person born of a woman but less than any person living in the kingdom [reign] of God, in Matthew 11:11.)

For Jesus, the kingdom [reign] of God was not a continuation of the current religious practices of Israel, which was what the Sadducees wanted; it was not the political restoration of Israel, which is what the Zealots wanted; it was not a Holy Commonwealth, which was what the Pharisees wanted; and it was not a cataclysmic intervention of God into human history, which was what apocalyptic literature wanted (e.g., Isaiah 24-27.) In Matthew 6:19-21 and Luke 12:16-21, Jesus warned His disciples not to spend their time and energy trying to create an earthly kingdom [reign] of God [a utopia] instead of spending their time and energy seeking heavenly treasures. Humanity cannot create the kingdom [reign] of God, because we cannot summon God into our utopia. So, for Judeo-Christian believers, the kingdom [reign] of God is God's gift to humanity. Jesus' ministry was focused on teaching His Father's will for us and on helping a suffering people: "All the longings of the Hebrew nation for freedom, peace, justice, and the fullness of life contained in the ancient covenant-promise were crystallized in this metaphor. <u>Only when God rules will the blessings of</u>

final shalom be realized... In taking up this metaphor and placing it in the center of his ministry, Jesus was taking up the hopes and expectations of his people."[37] In Matthew's Gospel, in His Sermon on the Mount, Jesus sketches how life will be in the kingdom [reign] of God by providing images of this new community through His teaching (e.g., Matthew 5:43-48.)

Third, Who is Invited into the Kingdom [Reign] of God

The OT and NT understanding of who is invited into the kingdom [reign] of God is difficult to separate from the concepts of a remnant and a Messiah, who will reign over God's kingdom. Israel's hopes for God's kingdom [reign] are described in prophetic literature, because Israel's prophets realized that their image of the kingdom [reign] of God had to change, that is, it could not include the entire nation of Israel, when many Israelites continually violated their covenant with YHWH. Instead, only a faithful, repentant remnant serving God would enter the kingdom [reign] of God.

The first prophet in prophetic literature, Amos, introduced the need for a good and faithful remnant in Israel in Amos 5:15. First Isaiah's prophecy went further in Isaiah 9:1-7; 11:1-9 and introduced the need for a new leader outside of Israel's succession of kings;

---

37 Zachary Hayes, *Visions of a Future*, 44

he would be a Messiah [God's anointed.] First Isaiah [Isaiah 1–39] reframed Israel's kingdom [reign] of God into a transfigured age of King David, which God would produce in the future. And one day in the future, there would appear a Messiah Prince in the line of King David, who would rule over this remnant. There would be a new David, a David redivivus, who would rule over a new and redeemed Israel, in Isaiah 9:1-7; 11:1-5; Micah 5:2-4.[38]

However, it was a new prophet, Second Isaiah [Isaiah 40–55], who spoke to the Israelites in captivity in Babylon and introduced a new theology about the kingdom [reign] of God and the Messiah. Israel's Messiah would not be King David redivivus; instead, he would be a vicarious suffering servant. The mission of the servant is described throughout Second Isaiah's suffering serving songs. For example, the new Messiah will return Israel to its original purpose of being a light to the nations and a witness to the glory of God, in Isaiah 49:6 "⁶he [God] says, 'It is too light a thing that you should be my servant to raise up the tribes of Jacob and to restore the survivors of Israel; I will give you as a light to the nations, that my salvation may reach to the end of the earth.'"

Israel's hopes for God's kingdom [reign] were changed again in apocalyptic literature (e.g., Isaiah

---

38 Bright, *The Kingdom of God*, 91

24-27.) The prophetic struggle throughout the OT was between Israel and the nations that ruled the world. However, the apocalyptic struggle was between God and the nations that ruled the world. In apocalyptic literature, God will cataclysmically enter the world, chastise His foes, and set up the kingdom [reign] of God. However, the Israelites did not always listen to or follow their prophets; so, when prophetic literature transmuted into apocalyptic literature, Israel did not listen again.

It should be noted that there were many changes in the concept of the kingdom [reign] of God as it passed from the OT to the NT. For example, "it (the kingdom [reign] of God) welcomes all humble, kindly men [and women] who "hunger and thirst" for it and who are willing to serve it to the utmost in Matt. 5:3-12; Luke 6:20-23). Wealth will not get anyone into the kingdom [reign] of God; indeed, wealth has kept many a person out (Mark 10:17-25). External rectitude [righteousness] is no ticket of admission; for that the scribes and Pharisees had in plenty, and it is certain that crooks and prostitutes will enter the Kingdom ahead of them (Matt. 21:31) ... Nor is the call of that Kingdom a call to honor or to victory, as the world understands those terms, but [a call] to utter self-denial... But those who are called, there is given nothing less than the Servant mission."[38] [John Bright, *The Kingdom of God*, 210]

For Mark and Matthew, the faithful, repentant remnant are not born into the kingdom [reign] of God; so, they are not an elite group within Israel. Instead, they are individuals who obey the radical calling of being faithful and obedient to God while living in a secular world. For W. W. Meissner SJ, Christian believers belong to the kingdom by reason of their relationship with Christ, which implies a new covenant between God and humanity that carried with it certain promises and hopes.[39]

For Christian believers, Jesus the Christ is the actualization of Second Isaiah's suffering servant songs, in Isaiah 42:1-4; 49:1-6; 50:4-9; 52:13–53:12. In my opinion, in the thesis statement of St. Paul's epistle to the Romans, we learn that faith in Jesus brings us salvation or entry into the kingdom of God, in Romans 1:16-17 "[16]For I am not ashamed of the gospel; it is the power of God for salvation to everyone who has faith, to the Jew first and also to the Greek. [17]For in it [the Gospel] the righteousness of God is revealed through faith for faith; as it is written, "The one who is righteous will live by faith.""

The Christian concept of the kingdom [reign] of God evolved over the two-thousand-year history of Christian theology. In his wonderful book *The Kingdom of God in History*, Benedict Viviano describes the many

---

39 W.W. Meissner, S.J., *Thy Kingdom Come*, 171

changes that occurred in the Christian understanding of the kingdom [reign] of God throughout this time.

Fourth, What Condition Must Occur to Permanently Bring About the Kingdom [reign] of God?

The OT theology of the "Day of the Lord" resonates with the Parousia [Jesus' second coming] in Christan theology. Catholic believers include the concept of the Parousia in our Nicene Creed: "He [the risen Jesus] will come again in glory to judge the living and the dead and his kingdom [reign] will have no end." For Christian believers, Jesus' second coming will permanently bring about the kingdom [reign] of God. Jesus explicitly told us that the kingdom [reign] of God is not within our grasp, in John 18:36 "[36]My kingdom is not from this world. If my kingdom were from this world, my followers would be fighting to keep me from being handed over to the Jews. But as it is, my kingdom is not from here." The apocalyptic chapters in the Synoptic Gospels in Mark 13:1-37; Matthew 24:1-44; and Luke 21:1-38 do not mention a glorious new Jerusalem, although the book of Revelation does mention a new Jerusalem in Revelation 21:2. In my opinion, the new Jerusalem should be understood as a metaphorical new Jerusalem, because the kingdom [reign] of God is not a place; it is a condition, where God's presence and love exercises dominion over all of God's theocentric creation (e.g., there is no temple in the new Jerusalem, in Revelation 21:22 "²²I saw no temple in the city, for its temple is the Lord God the Almighty and the Lamb.")

God gave humanity dominion over His theocentric creation in Genesis 1:26, 28. The OT and the NT both describe the necessary critical change in dominion that will permanently bring about the kingdom [reign] of God, and I want to briefly examine some OT and NT references that describe this necessary change in dominion.

The OT has at least three references to the necessary change in dominion. <u>First</u>, in Psalm 22:27-28 "²²All the ends of the earth shall remember and turn to the Lord; and all the families of the nations shall worship before him. ²⁸For <u>dominion</u> belongs to the Lord, and he rules over the nations." <u>Second</u>, in Isaiah 9:6 "⁶For a child has been born for us, a son given to us; <u>authority</u> [dominion] rests upon his shoulders; and he is named Wonderful Counselor, Mighty God, Everlasting Father, Prince of Peace." And <u>Third</u>, in Daniel 7:13-14 "¹³As I watched in the night visions; I saw one like a human being coming with the clouds of heaven. And he came to the Ancient One [God] and was presented before him. ¹⁴<u>To him was given dominion and glory and kingship</u>, that all peoples, nations, and languages should serve him. <u>His dominion is an everlasting dominion</u> that shall not pass away, and his kingship is one that shall never be destroyed." For Christian believers, Jesus is the one like a human being that Daniel saw; Jesus is the actualization of Isaiah 9:6; and Jesus, not the Ancient One, will judge the living and the dead.

The NT has at least three references to the necessary change in dominion. <u>First,</u> St. Paul described the necessary change in dominion in 1 Corinthians 15:28 "²⁸When all things are subjected to him [Jesus], then the Son himself will also be subjected to the one who put all things in subjection under him, so that God may be all in all." <u>Second,</u> in the letter to the Ephesians, we're told in Ephesians 1:20-23 "²⁰God put this power [our ability to know God] to work in Christ when he raised him from the dead and seated him at his right hand in the heavenly places, ²¹<u>far above all rule and authority and power and dominion,</u> and above every name that is named, not only in this age but also in the age to come. ²²And he has put all things under his feet and has made him the head over all things for the church, ²³which is his body, the fullness of him who fills all in all." And <u>Third,</u> in Revelation 1:6 "<u>to him [Jesus] be glory and dominion forever and ever.</u> Amen."

The underlying Greek word for kingdom, "basileia," can also be translated "dominion." In my opinion, this necessary change in dominion is the critical change that will bring about and sustain the kingdom [reign] of God. Despite humanity's ongoing attempts to create a utopia, the kingdom [reign] of God remains a gift from

God, because humanity is not capable of creating or sustaining the kingdom [reign] of God. The relationship between God and humanity will be complete for a faithful, repentant, remnant of the new people of God, both the living and the dead, and they will live eternally in the kingdom [the reign] [the dominion] of God. Jesus described eternal life to His disciples, including us, in John 17:3 "[3]And this is eternal life, that they may know you, the only true God, and Jesus Christ whom you have sent." This eternal knowledge of God the Father and Jesus the Son will happen in the kingdom [reign] of God.

Part Three:

Finding God's Presence and Love through God's Religious Tradition

Introduction

In part three of my book, I want to describe several ways to find God's presence and love within any religious community (e.g., by studying and understanding the music, liturgies, and traditions of the community.) However, I'm a practicing Catholic, so I worship God through the music, liturgies, and traditions of the Roman Catholic Church. For Catholic believers, Jesus established and sustains His holy Church as an organization that communicates the offer of grace and truth to its worldwide community of believers. In part three of my book, I am focusing on two elements of Catholic religious liturgies and tradition: <u>First</u>, in chapter six, I examine how to find God's presence and love in Catholic sacraments, and <u>Second</u>, in chapter seven, I examine how to find God's presence and love in the documents of Catholic tradition (e.g., in Catholic Ecumenical Councils, in Papal Encyclicals, and in Catholic Mystics.)

CHAPTER SIX

Finding God's Presence and Love in Catholic Sacraments

Introduction

What is a Catholic sacrament? "Sacraments are "powers that comes forth" from the Body of Christ, which is ever-living and life-giving. They are actions of the Holy Spirit at work in his Body, the Church. They are "the masterworks of God" in the new and everlasting covenant."[40] The seven sacraments of the Catholic Church help us find God's presence and love in our everyday lives by providing seven unique, ongoing opportunities to worship and glorify God through their beautiful liturgical celebrations. For example, for Catholic believers, in the liturgy of the sacrament of the Eucharist, the host becomes the transubstantiated body and blood of Jesus Christ, which brings God's presence,

---

40 "Catechism of the Catholic Church," article 1116

love, and communion into our hearts, into our Church, and through us into our communities.

The sacraments touch our lives through the power of the Holy Spirit. The Catholic Church's authority for sacramental theology is derived from scriptures (e.g., Matthew 18:18 provides the scriptural basis for the sacrament of Reconciliation.) The Catholic Church believes that sacraments increase meaning and strength in our lives because: "Sacraments are efficacious signs of grace instituted by Christ and entrusted to the Church, by which divine life is dispensed to us."[41] Sacramental theology is not an abstraction, because the sacraments provide concrete ways to find and celebrate God's presence and love in our lives, to welcome new parishioners into the Church, to reconcile parishioners, to steer the vocations of parishioners, and to support the Catholic Church.

The Catholic Church believes that Christ instituted the sacraments in order to help us achieve a better righteousness throughout the phases of our lives. I will briefly describe the seven sacraments of the Catholic Church: <u>First</u>, the sacraments of <u>Christian initiation</u> [Baptism, Confirmation, and the Eucharist]; <u>Second</u>, the sacraments of <u>Christian healing</u> [Reconciliation and the Anointing of the sick]; and <u>Third</u>, the sacraments of <u>Christian vocation</u> [Marriage and Holy Orders.]

---

41 "Catechism of the Catholic Church," article 1131

God's love is present in the Catholic sacraments of initiation [Baptism, Confirmation, and Holy Eucharist]

<u>The sacrament of Baptism</u> provides the gateway to all sacraments: "Through the holy Spirit, Baptism is a bath that purifies, justifies, and sanctifies."[42] For Catholic believers, through the sacrament of Baptism we become a new creation, <u>an adopted child of God, who partakes of divine nature,</u> as a member of the body of Christ, and a temple of the Holy Spirit.[43] For Catholic believers, all the sacraments require ecclesial faith; so, infant baptism occurs within the faith of the believing community; which confirms the Catholic belief that God's grace [God's presence and love] is always unmerited.

<u>The sacrament of Confirmation</u> completes baptismal grace. Roman Catholics are confirmed as older children or young adults by a Bishop in order to obtain new strength in the Holy Spirit, similar to the way that the apostles obtained new strength through the Holy Spirit on the day of the Pentecost in Acts 2:1-13. Catholics become more spiritually alive through the sacrament of Confirmation because they complete the process of being born from above (John 3:1-21.) "The fullness of Spirit was not intended to remain uniquely the Messiah's, but was intended to be communicated to

---

[42] "Catechism of the Catholic Church," article 1227

[43] "Catechism of the Catholic Church," article 1265

the whole messianic people."[44] In my opinion, we also need to reconfirm our belief in Jesus throughout our lives.

For Catholic believers, the gifts and fruits of the Holy Spirit are identified in the Catechism of the Catholic Church; they're derived from the attributes of Jesus, and they're intended to help us achieve a better righteousness. The gifts of the Holy Spirit continually inform us of God's presence and love for us and they continually guide us through: wisdom, understanding, counsel, fortitude, knowledge and piety, and fear [reverence] of the Lord.[45] The fruits of the Holy Spirit continually inform us of God's presence and love for us by guiding us with: charity, joy, peace, patience, kindness, goodness, generosity, gentleness, faithfulness, modesty, self-control, and chastity.[46]

The sacraments of Baptism and Confirmation help Catholics to avoid being enslaved by the lower passions (e.g., the appetites.) Catholic believers are able to live in a new realm; the powers of sin and death are still present but through the grace of the sacraments, Catholics come closer to the dominion of God, which is marked by righteousness and holiness. St. Paul tells us

---

44 "Catechism of the Catholic Church," article 1286, 1287

45 "Catechism of the Catholic Church," article 1831

46 "Catechism of the Catholic Church," article 1832

the consequences of continually refusing God's offer of grace in Romans 1:24 "Therefore God gave them up in the lusts of their hearts to impurity, to the degrading of their bodies among themselves."

<u>The sacrament of Holy Eucharist</u> provides: "the source and summit of Christian life," because <u>it directly nourishes us with God's presence and love</u>.[47] The Eucharist connects our faith to the "Last Supper," as a memorial of Jesus' suffering, death, resurrection, and ascension. The Gospels, Mark 14:22-25; Matthew 26:26-29; Luke 22:14-20; John 6, and 1 Corinthians 11:23-26, describe the institution of the sacrament of Holy Eucharist, but their manifold descriptions are too detailed for this book.

Practicing Catholics gather for Mass weekly, on designated Holy Days, and on sacramental liturgical celebrations (e.g., Baptism, Confirmation, Marriage.) The Mass consists of two major liturgies: <u>First</u>, the liturgy of the Word, which includes readings from the OT and the NT and <u>Second</u>, the liturgy of the Eucharist, which has three major components: <u>First</u>, the offertory, where we offer our gifts and prayers to God; <u>Second</u>, the consecration, where our gifts of bread and wine are transubstantiated into the body and blood of Jesus Christ; and <u>Third</u>, holy communion, where we receive the transubstantiated body and blood of Jesus Christ

---

[47] "Catechism of the Catholic Church," article 1324

in the form of a host and/or wine. For Catholics, the Eucharist, is also called Holy Communion, because through this sacrament, Catholic believers obtain communion on at least three different levels: First, communion with Jesus; Second, communion with the Church and its members; and Third, communion with our brothers and sisters outside the Church through our example, because we make God's grace [God's presence and love] visible to others.

God's love is present in the Catholic sacraments of healing [Reconciliation and the Anointing of the sick]

The sacrament of Reconciliation is also called confession. Catholic believers go to confession because we need to reconciled with God, the Church, and the Church community in order to sustain God's presence and love in our lives. The successful completion of the sacrament of Confession requires several steps: First, we confess our sins to a priest; Second, we make an act of contrition, that is, we confess our sorrow for our sins and repent, or agree to change our lives; Third, our sins are forgiven by a priest through absolution, because the priest is God's representative on earth; Fourth, we complete our penance; and Fifth, we're reconciled back into the sanctity of the Church. For Catholic believers, the sacrament of Reconciliation [confession] provides a continual opportunity to obtain the abundant life that Jesus wants us to have, in John 10:10, both in our current situation and in eternity.

<u>The sacrament of Anointing</u> is often administered to a dying person, but it can be received by Catholic believers in danger from any health risk. In receiving the sacrament of Anointing, we are uniting ourselves with the Paschal Mystery of Christ [the suffering, death, resurrection, ascension, and glorification of Christ.] For Catholic believers, the communion of saints intercedes for the benefit of the sick person, who in turn contributes to the sanctification of the Church by obtaining God's gift of grace [God's presence and love.] The sacrament of Anointing can forgive sins when confession is not possible, and prepare a person to pass over into eternal life.

God's love is present in the Catholic sacraments of vocation [Matrimony and Holy Orders]

<u>The sacrament of Matrimony</u> is intended to allow people to form a life partnership ordered for the good of the spouses (e.g., for the procreation and education of their children.) For Catholics, this covenant was elevated to the dignity of a sacrament by Christ in Matthew 5:31-32; therefore, the intent of the sacrament of Matrimony is to create an exclusive and permanent bond between the spouses.

<u>The sacrament of Holy Orders</u> anoints Catholics to continue the mission entrusted by Christ to His

Church. The sacrament of Holy Orders occurs in three degrees: First, to the episcopate [a Bishop]; Second, to the presbyterate [a priest]; and Third, to the Deaconate [a Deacon.] In the sacrament of Holy Orders, the recipient is consecrated and receives God's blessing. For Catholic believers, Christ is the only true priest. So, individuals who receive the sacrament of Holy Orders are considered ordained ministers of the Church, who make the grace of Jesus Christ [God's presence and love] more accessible to believers.

CHAPTER SEVEN

Finding God's Presence and Love in Catholic Tradition

Introduction

How does Catholic tradition help us to find God's presence and love? The Catholic Church is not a collection of beautiful cathedrals that have arisen over two millennia. The Catholic Church consists of communities of faith throughout the world whose parishioners have become part of God's new remnant, because they are the righteous fruit of Jesus Christ. How does the Catholic Church bring about a community of God? The Catholic Church establishes communities of faith that touch people everywhere in the world through its missionaries and their ministries. Today, following Jesus' commission in Matthew 28:19-20; John 20:21; and Acts 1:8, the Catholic Church brings the Word of God to a billion constituents around the world. The core beliefs of the Catholic Church are defined in the Nicene Creed. Therefore, the Catholic Church is a collection of like-minded believers who have chosen to follow Jesus as their personal Lord and Savior, because they believe that Jesus is the mediator of their faith and a bridge [full of grace and truth] between humanity and divinity.

Has Catholic tradition changed over two millennia? Yes, Catholic tradition has evolved and been updated over two millennia. In my opinion, the Catholic Church evolved through at least six major historical stages: <u>First</u>, Christianity started as a sect of Judaism [ca. 35-70]; <u>Second</u>, Christianity became a distinct religion and Church after the second Jewish Diaspora [ca. 70]; <u>Third</u>, Christianity became the official religion of the Roman Empire beginning with the Roman Emperor Constantine the Great [after the Council of Nicaea [around 325]] and finalized under Roman Emperor Theodosius [ca. 380]; <u>Fourth</u>, Christianity evolved into Christendom (after the dissolution of the Roman Empire [ca. 476], because Europe considered Christian nations as one large church-state, called Christendom); <u>Fifth</u>, there was a schism between the eastern and western Catholic churches [ca. 1054]; and <u>Sixth</u>, there was a schism between Catholics and Protestants called the Protestant Reformation [ca. 1500.] Throughout these distinct periods of Christianity, Catholic theology evolved (e.g., today, the Catholic Church provides <u>principles</u> for reflection, <u>criteria</u> to exercise judgment, and <u>norms</u> for believers.) The Catholic Church accomplishes its mission through their Magisterium, their Ecumenical Councils, their Papal Encyclicals, their theologians, their saints, and their mystics, because no individual Catholic Church community could generate norms for a billion worldwide believers.

Finding God's Presence and Love in the Documents of Catholic Ecumenical Councils

In addition to Catholic sacraments, Catholics believers are blessed with the documents from twenty-one Ecumenical Councils written over two millennia (e.g., in the documents of Vatican II we find Lumen Gentium [Light of the Nations.]) Finding God's presence and love in the documents of Catholic Ecumenical Councils is similar to studying any discipline; that is, we need to study with good teachers, work at understanding the theology in the documents, and transcend our education by using our knowledge and gifts to help others. Throughout these documents, we can find God's presence and love (e.g., in new social ethics at critical times in western civilization.)

I'm going to limit my comments to some of the impacts of two of the Catholic Church's twenty-one Ecumenical Councils: <u>First</u>, brief references to the documents from the Council of Trent [1545–1563] and second, brief references to the documents from the Second Vatican Council [1962–1965.]

First, God's love is present in the documents of the Council of Trent, which addressed the impact to the Catholic Church and its parishioners caused by the Protestant Reformation. The Council of Trent lasted eighteen years and the Council's documents offer moral teaching to Catholic believers, because the Church is an expert in humanity but not the only expert. So, the Church and its teaching should be understood as neither a spectator nor a dictator in human morality.

The Council of Trent changed its theology and its practices regarding many issues raised by Luther: First, the Council of Trent reformed its practice of pastoral ministry (e.g., the Council called for Bishops to reside in their diocese and perform their specific duties there and the Council called for establishing seminaries, which established standards to preach God's Word) and Second, the Council responded to Luther's doctrines (e.g., on salvation.) The Council established the doctrine of Justification by faith, which basically means sinners are declared to be righteous in the sight of God through their faith just as if they never sinned. The Council carefully responded to Luther with theology that avoided Pelagianism (e.g., salvation depends on human effort) and Manicheism and Gnosticism (e.g., salvation depends on special hidden knowledge.)

God's love is present in the documents of the Second Vatican Council, which addressed the impacts on western civilization from two world wars, fascism, NAZI totalitarianism, and the death camps in Europe. The Second Vatican Council dramatically shifted the function of the Church in society in several ways: First, instead of speaking to the world, the Church began to listen and to learn from the world; Second, the Church's perspective is now understood as operating in the present and the future, not just in the past; and Third, the Church focused on people and their actions living in their personal environment as opposed to the Church's previous impersonal view of Catholic social ethics guided by natural law.

We can find God's presence and love throughout the documents of Vatican Two. I'm going to briefly examine one of the documents from Vatican II: Lumen Gentium [Light of the Nations.] The Council acknowledged the necessity for the Catholic Church and its believers to become a light to people, who live in a world full of emotions, temptations, dichotomies, incongruities, evil, and the fear of death. In the opening words of Lumen Gentium, we're told: "Christ is the light of humanity; and it is, accordingly, the heart-felt desire of this sacred Council being gathered together in the Holy Spirit, that, by proclaiming the Gospel to every creature (cf. Mark 16:15), it may bring to all men that light [truth] of Christ, which shines out visibly from the Church."[48] Throughout Lumen Gentium, the Council defined the role of the Pilgrim Church of Christ (e.g., the clerical hierarchy and the laity), to become Christ's presence on earth, that is, a light to the nations. Catholic believers are called to bring God's presence and love to others (e.g., through our example and through our ministries) until the kingdom [reign] of God finally delivers people from the slavery of sin in Romans 8:18-21 and from "the heart-ache and the thousand natural shocks that flesh is heir to." (*Hamlet*, Act III, Scene 1, William Shakespeare)

Lumen Gentium also included a brief discussion about Mary, the Mother of the Catholic Church. Marian spirituality and tradition have always been central in the Catholic Church, because Mary is the Mother of God [Theotokos.] The Virgin Mary, who at the message of an angel received the Word of God in her heart and gave life to the world through Jesus, is acknowledged and honored as being truly the Mother of God... The Catholic Church, taught by the Holy Spirit, honors her with filial affection and devotion as a most beloved mother... who occupies a place in the Church which is the highest after Christ and also closest to us.[49]

---

48 Vatican Council II, Volume 1, Lumen Gentium, "The Conciliar and Post Council Documents, New Revised Edition", 350

49 Vatican Council II, Volume 1, Lumen Gentium, "The Conciliar and Post Council Documents, New Revised Edition", pg. 414; (cf. Paul VI, Allocution to the Council, 4 December 1963: AAS 56 (1964), p. 414

We receive God's grace [God's presence and love] here and now, but God's grace will be perfected in us in the renewal of all things, in Acts 3:19-21. So, until the renewal of all things is realized, the Pilgrim Church, including its theology, its sacraments, its tradition, and its institutions, belongs to the present age of emotions, temptations, dichotomies, incongruities, evil, and the fear of death. Today, Catholic believers need to profess their belief in Jesus Christ regardless of the marginalization or persecution that we may receive from the secular world, because we believe that the Church and its members will always be strengthened by God's grace (e.g., Hebrews 13:5 "I will never leave you or forsake you.") In writing Lumen Gentium, Vatican II followed Vatican I in declaring Jesus Christ as the eternal pastor of the Catholic Church, which He entrusted to His apostles in John 20:21 "[21]Jesus said to them again, 'Peace be with you. As the Father has sent me, so I send you.'"

Finding God's Presence and Love in Papal Encyclicals

Introduction

In addition to finding God's presence and love [grace] in Catholic sacraments and Catholic ecumenical councils, the Catholic Church has a rich history of popes solving theological and practical problems that affect its parishioners throughout two millennia of

Christianity by writing Papal Encyclicals (e.g., Rerum Novarum [of new things] published in 1891.) How do Papal Encyclicals help us find God's presence and love? For Catholic believers, we can find God's presence and love in Papal Encyclicals because we believe that they contain experiences and instructions that increase our faith in God while we live in a secular world. Papal Encyclicals continue to impact international politics (e.g., the Catholic Church's idea of a just wage resonates today in America and Europe.)

The early Catholic Church based its social ethics on the New Testament belief that the kingdom [reign] of God was imminent. So, the Church emphasized the spiritual development of the followers of Christ (e.g., Christians were told to focus on the love of God and neighbors, which is consistent with the ethics of the OT [e.g., Deut. 6:4-9; Lev. 19:18.]) The medieval Catholic Church modified the emphasis of early Christian ethics through the writings of St. Thomas Aquinas [1225-1274.] Aquinas was influenced by Aristotle's ethics [384-322 BCE] and Zeno's stoic ethics [334-262 BCE] and to some extent he incorporated their ethics into the Catholic Church. The Church's medieval modifications to Christian ethics dominated until Vatican II [1962–1965.] For Aquinas, there were four kinds of law: First, the eternal law of God, which is evident in creation; Second, natural law, which interprets God's eternal law by understanding our human nature and the inherent rights conferred on us by God, by nature, and by reason, not by acts of legislation (e.g., our freedom); Third, divine law, which is the law of the Catholic Church; and Fourth, civil law, which must be in harmony with natural law. The modern-day Catholic Church focuses on people living in their personal environment as opposed to the Church's previous impersonal view of Catholic social ethics guided by natural law.

Pope Leo XIII's Papal Encyclical Rerum Novarum [of New Things]

How do Papal Encyclicals theologically and practically address existing problems in society? Papal Encyclicals are one of the mechanisms that the Church uses to change its theological perspective or to create new theological perspectives. In the 1700–1800's, the Catholic Church necessarily reached out to society because of the dramatic changes to western civilization caused by two industrial revolutions. It became necessary to instruct Catholics through Papal Encyclicals in order to increase their awareness of God's presence and love in their world and in their lives. Pope Leo XIII [1810–1903] wrote Papal Encyclicals to respond to the impacts of the first industrial revolution [1750–1850] and the second industrial revolution [1870–1914], especially his famous 1891 papal encyclical, Rerum Novarum [of new things.]

There were a myriad of background forces that guided Pope Leo XIII in writing Rerum Novarum, including: First, the shift from feudalism to the industrial revolution; Second, the shift from monarchies to constitutional monarchies; Third, increased population after the bubonic plague passed [1340-1400]; Fourth, improved farming technology; Fifth, burgeoning urbanization and the emergence of the bourgeoise class; and Sixth, improved manufacturing technology (e.g., the home and the family were previously engaged in the production, transformation, and consumption of goods; however, after the industrial revolutions the production and transformation of goods moved out of the home, which led people to trade their uncertain farming life for low paying but stable jobs in squalid urban centers.)

Rerum Novarum addressed the displacement of people caused by the industrial revolutions and the resulting new social order (e.g., the need for just wages, the need to form trade unions, the right to private property, and free enterprise.) Quadragesima Anno [in the fortieth year] was written forty years after Rerum Novarum in 1931 by Pope Pius XI in order to speak to the social changes caused by WWI and the Great Depression. Quadragesima Anno discussed the attack on capitalism (e.g., wealth being concentrated in a few hands); however, socialism and communism were never considered legitimate alternatives to democracy and capitalism (e.g., Quadragesima Anno called for a just wage that allowed a man to support his family but not a wage that crippled business.) The documents from papal encyclicals are designed to clarify the Church's position on difficult practical and theological issues and to showcase God's presence and love in every age.

Finding God's Presence and Love in the Documents of Catholic Mystics

Reading Catholic mystics may seem like an improbable place to find God's presence and love and it certainly will not appeal to everyone, but it might help someone to find some of the answers that they are searching for (e.g., St. Edith Stein, a Jewish woman, read St. Teresa of Avila's magnificent book *The Interior Castle* and sometime later asked to be baptized into the Catholic Church. Edith Stein was baptized in 1922; however, the NAZIs took her out of her convent and murdered her in Auschwitz-Birkenau in 1942.[50])

What is the point of Catholic mysticism? Some people are blessed to experience a mystical revelation from God. Even though we may never personally receive a mystical experience, we can still find God's presence and love in the writings of the Christian mystics over two millennia of Christianity. What is a

---

50   Florent Gaboriau, *The Conversion of Edith Stein*, 15-19

mystical experience from God? A mystical experience is a conscious and profound union between God and a person. Mystical experiences require a deeper loving personal relationship with God than most of us are able to achieve in this life. We need to somehow reach the mystical relationship that St. Paul had with Jesus, in Galatians 2:20 "²⁰it is no longer I who live, but it is Christ who lives in me."

Mystical revelation, like all revelation, must be understood in a way that allows us as readers to find God's presence and love in their revelations. The Christian mystics that I've selected achieve that goal. I will briefly review the writings of several Christian mystics in three different historical periods of the Catholic Church: <u>First</u>, the mystical experiences recorded in the NT; <u>Second</u>, the mystical experiences recorded in the sixteenth century Catholic Church; and <u>Third</u>, the mystical experiences recorded in the modern-day Catholic Church.

The Mystical Experiences Recorded in the NT

In his epistles, St. Paul testified at least three times about his personal mystical experiences of God's presence and love during his lifetime: <u>First,</u> St. Paul described his mystical conversion experience in Galatians 1:11-24, which the book of Acts also described in Acts 9:1-19 and repeated in Acts 22:6-21; 26:12-23;

Second, St. Paul defended his ministry to the Corinthian Church in 1 Corinthians 9:1b "Have I not seen Jesus our Lord?"; and Third, in my opinion, St. Paul's strongest testimony about his mystical experiences is described in 2 Corinthians 12:2-4 "²I know a person in Christ who fourteen years ago was caught up to the third heaven—whether in the body or out of the body I do not know; God knows. ³And I know that such a person—whether in the body or out of the body I do not know; God knows—⁴was caught up into Paradise and heard things that are not to be told, that no mortal is permitted to repeat." In my opinion, St. Paul was describing his own personal mystical experiences.

In my opinion, the individual and group resurrection experiences of the risen Jesus recorded in all four Gospels and in Paul's epistles were mystical experiences for Jesus' apostles and disciples (e.g., Mark 16:1-18; Matthew 28:1-20; Luke 24:13-49; John 20:11-29; Acts 1:1-5.) And many of Jesus' apostles and disciples had an additional mystical experience when they witnessed Jesus' ascension to His Father in Mark 16:19-20; Luke 24:50-53; and Acts 1:6-11. In my opinion, when the risen Jesus appeared to His apostles the second time in John's Gospel, a mystical experience, and asked His apostle Thomas to put his finger in the holes in His hands and his hand in His side, Thomas made the strongest confession of faith in the NT regarding Jesus' identity, in John 20:27-28. "²⁷Then he said to Thomas,

'Put your finger here and see my hands. Reach out your hand and put it in my side. Do not doubt but believe.' [28]Thomas answered him, 'My Lord and my God!'" St. Paul summarized the extent of Jesus' resurrection appearances [mystical experiences] in 1 Corinthians 15:3-8 "[3]For I handed on to you as of first importance what I in turn had received: that Christ died for our sins in accordance with the scriptures, [4]and that he was buried, and that he was raised on the third day in accordance with the scriptures, [5]and that he appeared to Cephas, then to the twelve. [6]Then he appeared to more than five hundred brothers and sisters at one time, most of whom are still alive, though some have died. [7]Then he appeared to James, then to all the apostles. [8]Last of all, as to one untimely born, he appeared also to me."

The Mystical Experiences Recorded in the Sixteenth Century Catholic Church

While there were many mystical experiences recorded in the sixteenth century Christian Church, I want to focus on two specific Catholic saints: <u>First</u>, St. John of the Cross and <u>Second</u>, St. Teresa of Avila.

<u>St. John of the Cross [1542-1591] was blessed with the immanent presence and love of God</u> and he described his mystical experience as the dark night of the soul, because the dark night of the soul necessarily preceded

his mystical experience. For St. John of the Cross, we live in darkness; therefore, we need God's light [truth] to fully understand anything, in John 1:5 "⁵The light shines in the darkness, and the darkness did not overcome it." St. John of the Cross described his journey into "the dark night of the soul," where the sensory and spiritual parts of the soul were turned back to Adam's state of innocence in order to find a mystical union with God's presence and love. St. John told us that we can find this blessed union with God by escaping from ourselves and our enemies in the darkness of night using the sacred ladder of love. The dark night is a necessary step in our transformation for union with God. The painful privation of the dark night includes the darkness of our intellect and a disconnection from all our possessions, which provides the soul with a new fervor for service to God through God's grace [God's presence and love.]

St. John of the Cross moved beyond the "dark night of the soul" to a more complete mystical union with God, which he described as "the living flame of love." In this more perfect mystical experience of God, a deeper love was revealed to him. St. John told us that we can journey toward this participation with God but: "No one attains to this blessing except through an intimate nakedness, purgation, and spiritual hiding from all that is of creatures."[51] Neither our feelings nor

---

51 Kieran Kavanaugh, OCD, *The Collected Works of St. John of the Cross*, 454

our intellect can understand the nature of God, who remains Absolute Mystery; therefore, we must journey to God in love, because <u>the love of God is deeper than the knowledge of God.</u> Our journey ends in God, but not because we have as much capacity as God; rather, it's because our limited soul becomes more like God. In other words, through a better righteousness, we can achieve a mystical experience that brings us closer to God's presence and love.

St. John of the Cross described the wonders of the force of love in his life using an analogy about rocks and souls being drawn to their deepest centers. The deepest center of any object is the farthest point that the object can attain through its own being and power; so, the deepest center of a rock is the center of the earth oriented by the force of gravity. Similarly, the deepest center of a human being is God oriented by the force of love. "The soul's center is God… love is the inclination, strength, and power for the soul in making its way to God, for love unites it with God."[52] As we journey home to God, we need to remember that the many forms of restlessness that we experience in our daily lives (e.g., our questions, our disappointments) are caused by God's love for us. So, we continually need to thank God for our gift of restlessness and for our gift of abstraction because they provide us with an opportunity to find

---
52 Kieran Kavanaugh, OCD, *The Collected Works of St. John of the Cross*, 645

God's presence and love in our daily lives and to find our way home to God.

St. Teresa of Avila [1515-1582] was blessed with the immanent presence and love of God. St. Teresa was born in Avila, Spain, in 1515 and St. John of the Cross was her Father confessor. To say that St. Teresa lived in a world that discriminated against women barely describes her situation (e.g., St. Teresa was not allowed to study theology, because she was a woman and St. Teresa lived during the Inquisition, where anything controversial could result in punishment or death.) In addition, St. Teresa had few, if any, female role models to guide her spiritual journey. Still, she found a way to write hundreds of letters and poems and four books including her *The Interior Castle*. "One of her early biographers, Fr. Diego de Yepes, testified that Teresa told him that on the evening of Trinity Sunday, 1577, God showed her in a flash the whole book."[53]

St. Teresa gives us detailed information about her mystical journey into her "Interior Castle." However, like all mystics, St. Teresa is trying to make the ineffable effable. Her spiritual journey occurred through seven stages of prayer, where she saw her soul as a castle made of diamond or crystal. She passed through each stage of prayer, or through each mansion in her castle, until she finally reached the innermost mansion in her interior

---

53 Kieran Kavanaugh OCD, Rodriquez, Otilia OCD, *The Collected Works of St. Teresa of Avila*, Volume Two, 268

castle and found God's dwelling place, that is, God's presence and love alive within her. I'll briefly examine the seven stages of prayer that St. Teresa described. St. Teresa emphasized that the most difficult part of the journey is finding the entry point into our own interior castle, which we can only find by listening to God (e.g., Mark 9:7 "This is my Son, the Beloved; listen to him!")

The first and second mansions are purgative, where we are cleansed from sin by non-physical mortifications (e.g., good works, prayer, and meditation.) For St. Teresa, the first mansion is the hardest mansion to find, because worldly cares and distractions compete to keep us out. We see darkness in the first mansion caused by all the distractions that we bring in with us. To move to the second mansion, we must give up all unnecessary things and appreciate the riches of a mature spiritual life. In the first two mansions, God communicates with us externally (e.g., through conversations, sermons, books, feelings, and thoughts.) We must resolve to seek God and not ourselves: "We are called to love God above all things with our whole heart and soul and mind. Love is not a mood of delight or contentment, it's not a warm fuzzy feeling, and it is not an inner glow. Love is choosing – it is choosing to love God even though our conscious being feels no attraction save for what is here and now desirable."[54]

---

54 Ruth Burrows, *Fire Upon the Earth*, 23

The third and fourth mansions are illuminative; they help us become passive and help us to find God in our interior castle. The souls that enter the third mansion are trying not to offend God even in minor ways (e.g., venial sins.) They spend their time well, like Jesus did while He was on earth, for example, helping their neighbor. We're rewarded in the third mansion, because the Lord gives us consolations far greater than the comforts and distractions in life. For St. Teresa, "The way through the interior castle is the way of Jesus; his vision, his values, his fortitude, and his constancy, and these often seem alien to the conscious self."[55] The fourth mansion is the transition mansion where the natural meets the supernatural and spiritual delights begin in God and end in self. Here we meet God! Teresa used the metaphor of two troughs of water to explain the fourth mansion: the first trough comes from far away through a system of aqueducts (e.g., consolations drawn from meditation) but the other trough has its source of water in the immediate presence and love of God. We must prepare to receive God in person, but God doesn't reveal His presence and love to us until we're able to recognize it. We need to approach God like Simeon and Anna approached the baby Jesus in Luke's Gospel, in Luke 2:25-38, and we need to maintain our

---

55 Ruth Burrows, *Fire Upon the Earth*, 71

focus on God and not substitute our own version of the golden calf.

<u>The fifth, sixth, and seventh mansions are unitive</u> but we must get beyond the pull of earthliness. St. Teresa experienced a profound presence of God's love, when she experienced God loving her, which she called "light on" mystical experiences. Even though we probably won't find union with God's presence and love in a "light on" experience, we can find God's offer of grace [God's presence and love.]

In <u>the fifth mansion</u> we must really decide if we want union with God, because we must make a transition from a caterpillar to a butterfly. In other words, we need to die to ourselves and surrender to God in order to find union with God. However, our union with God is only a visit and not a permanent abiding with God. The silkworm must die and we ourselves must put the silkworm to death (e.g., once a silkworm is grown it begins to build the house where it will die.) For Christians, that house is Jesus Christ, in Galatians 2:20. In <u>the sixth mansion</u> we're admitted into the unspeakable riches of Christ, but God still leaves us in our own human nature for our greater good. St. Teresa is wounded with love and God must have everything. St. Teresa explains favors, sufferings, and raptures that occur in the sixth mansion, but they are too detailed for this book. She explains that all of her previous experiences were designed to wrench her away from self and bring her into the seventh mansion: "The seventh mansion is Jesus, he living in us and we in him, the perfection of marriage."[56] When we choose to open ourselves up to God, we become what we're intended to become, in Ephesians 1:5 "He destined us for adoption as his children through Jesus Christ, according to the good pleasure of his will." When the soul is brought into the seventh mansion, the soul is in unity with God, like two wax candles that produce one flame. The seventh mansion is the end of our long, prayerful journey. We're home, just like St. Paul described in Galatians 2:20 "It is no longer I who live, but it is Christ who lives in me." We need to remember that very few people reach mystical unity with God during their lifetime. St. Teresa explained that if we are able to reach unity with God, we don't lose our individuality, interests, preferences, or emotions. Instead, when we find Jesus in our interior castle, we become fully human; that is, we find abundant life in Jesus by becoming a self for others, because our salvation comes from loving God by loving our neighbor. In the Gospels, Jesus' apostles wanted to sit at His right hand and His left hand in eternity but Jesus told them that it was not His to grant and that they were looking for the wrong things.

---

56 Ruth Burrows, *Fire Upon the Earth*, 110

Instead of being self-serving, they needed to become a self-for-others (e.g., Mark 10:35-45; Matthew 20:20-28.)

The Mystical Experiences Recorded in the Modern-Day Catholic Church

While there are many mystical experiences recorded in the modern-day Catholic Church, I want to focus on two specific modern day Catholic mystics: <u>first</u>, Karl Rahner SJ, a Jesuit priest and <u>second</u>, Thomas Merton, a Trappist monk.

<u>For Rahner, our humanity is actualized in several ways</u>: <u>First</u>, through God's ex nihilo creative act; <u>Second</u>, through God's presence, love, and communication in our self-transcendence; and <u>Third</u>, in our innermost being through the immanent presence of the Holy Spirit. By accepting the offer of God's grace, which Rahner calls "the supernatural existential," God's love becomes present to us. And God's presence and love comes closer to us than we are to ourselves, in Romans 8:26-27, because prior to accepting God's offer of grace, God's love was already present to us in a theocentric world permeated with the offer of God's grace. The transcendent experience of God's presence and love [God's amazing grace] is often unthematic, that is, we don't realize that we're in God's presence and love and God's grace is always asymptotic, because the reality of Absolute Mystery cannot disclose itself to us in the

same way that sense experience discloses an object to us, because God is Spirit, in John 4:24. Nevertheless, grace is radically rooted in the depths of human beings and it constitutes our human dignity.

For Rahner the priest, the teacher, and the mystic, God's presence and love can be experienced in every part of our daily lives, because the mystery we find in the details of our lives is the offer of God's grace that permeates the world. In his biography of Karl Rahner, Herbert Vorgrimler cited a wonderful quote from Rahner about Rahner's own mystical experiences of God's presence and love: "I have experienced God directly. I have experienced God, the nameless and unfathomable one, the one who is silent and yet near, in the trinity of his approach to me. I have really encountered God, the true and living one, the one for whom this name that quenches all names is fitting. God himself. I have experienced God himself, not human words about him. This experience is not barred to anyone. I want to communicate it to others as well as I can."[57]

For Rahner, we're oriented toward God's presence love and we remain free to love God, self, and others. We experience God's deepest presence and love in our lives by understanding our own experience. Rahner explains this in his book, *Foundations of Christian Faith*: "If man

---

[57] Herbert Vorgrimler, *Understanding Karl Rahner*, 11

really is a subject, that is, a transcendent, responsible free being who as subject is both entrusted into his own hands and always in the hands of what is beyond his control, then basically this has already said that man is a being oriented toward God. His orientation towards the absolute mystery always continues to be offered to him by this mystery as the ground and content of his being."[58]

Thomas Merton, a Trappist monk, was a mystic of contemplative prayer. Merton tried to teach us how to become more aware of God's presence and love in our lives through contemplative prayer. For Merton, the seeds of contemplation are planted in us every day, especially the seeds of the Word of God, in Mark 4:14-20, because God's love is present to us every moment of every day. We need to accept and nourish the seeds of contemplation that are planted in us in order to become our true selves in both our identity and our happiness. But to find our deepest consciousness, our true selves, we need to empty our Cartesian selves [I think therefore I am] through a human kenosis. Then we can recognize God's presence and love in our innermost "I," where the seeds of contemplation are planted and where they need to be harvested.[59]

---

[58] Karl Rahner SJ, *Foundations of Christian Faith*, 44

[59] Thomas Merton OCSO, *New Seeds of Contemplation*, 13

Merton described love as the reason for our existence, because God is love, in 1 John 4:8, 16. "To say I am made in the image of God is to say that love is the reason for my existence, for God is love. Love is my true identity. Selflessness is my true self. Love is my true character."[60] We're only able to find our true selves when we're transported in one degree or another more deeply into God's presence and love. We come closest to God's presence and love at the deepest level of our consciousness by concentrating on God's presence and love (e.g., by removing unnecessary distractions from our lives.) Contemplative prayer, like all prayer, is surrendering to God in love in order to become our true selves, and this can only occur after we believe in God, trust in God, and recognize that we're radically dependent on God for our happiness, fulfillment, and salvation. Merton reminds us that God's presence and love can be found in our deepest consciousness, which St. Paul confirmed in Galatians 2:20 "It is no longer I who live, but it is Christ who lives in me."

---

60 Thomas Merton OCSO, *New Seeds of Contemplation*, 60

Part Four:
Responding to God's Presence and Love As Individuals

Introduction

In the previous three parts of my book, I described several ways to find and understand God's presence and love in our everyday lives. In part four of my book, I acknowledge that there are innumerable ways to respond to God's offer of grace and I describe at least ten ways to individually respond to God's presence and love in our everyday lives. Once we've experienced and accepted God's offer of grace in our lives, we become equipped to develop a faithful, positive, loving, personal relationship with God. However, even though we find God's presence and love [God's offer of grace] in our lives, we still experience the everyday difficulties of life including: our emotions, temptations, dichotomies, incongruities, evil, and the fear of death. Despite our everyday difficulties, we need to find a way to individually respond to God that focuses on what God wants from us, in Hosea 6:6 "⁶For I desire steadfast love and not sacrifice, the knowledge of God rather than burnt offerings."

In order to develop and sustain our personal relationship with God, we need to acknowledge that we're created by God; we have a designed orientation toward God; and our destination is to return home to God. For example, in Genesis 5:24 "²⁴Enoch walked with God; then he was no more, because God took him." Whether we understand that God took Enoch while he was alive or after he was dead, either way, Enoch walked with God, because <u>God took him</u>. God's presence and love will help us to lead our lives in a way that ends like Enoch's life, that is, <u>God will take us</u>. We may be unsure of our destination but Jesus knows where our destination is, because that's what He told His apostles, in John 14:3 "I go and prepare a place for you I will come and take you to myself that where I am you also may be." However, we need to respond to God with a better righteousness, in Matthew 5:20, because Jesus is preparing a place for us.

Christians believe that we have an internal covenant with God written into our hearts, as the major Israelite prophets prophesied in Jeremiah 31:31-34; Ezekiel 11:19-20; 36:26-27; and Isaiah 63:11-13 around the time of the first Diaspora. For Christian believers, Jesus fulfills their prophecies and gives us an advocate, His Holy Spirit to help us, in John 14:16-17, 25-26; 15:26; 16:7; and 1 John 2:1-2. The gift of the indwelling Holy Spirit in our deepest consciousness helps us to accept God's offer of grace and nourish the seeds of God's gifts, which leads us to concrete actions that develop a better righteousness (e.g., by asking for God's help in Matthew 7:7-8; 18:19-20; Luke 11:9-13; John 11:21-23; 14:13-14; 15:7,16; 16:23-24; James. 1:5-8; 1 John 3:21-22; 5:14-15.) God is holy and righteous; so, if we want to hang out with

God, we need to become more holy (e.g., Psalms 51:9-10; Romans 12:1-2) and more righteousness (e.g., Matthew 5–7.) If we give away our power to become more holy and more righteous, then we're denying God's offer of grace in our daily lives.[61] In my opinion, salvation doesn't mean we're living in a pleasure-filled paradise; it means that we're living with a better righteousness, that is, we are conforming to the will of God and we are receiving God's hidden treasures in our lives. We're able to do this through God's mercy and love, but we need to trust God with the same conviction that St. Paul trusted God, in Romans 8:38-39 "[38]For I am convinced that neither death, nor life, nor angels, nor rulers, nor things present, nor things to come, nor powers, "[39]nor height, nor depth, nor anything else in all creation, will be able to separate us from the love of God in Christ Jesus our Lord."

---

61 Bill Huesbsch, *A New Look at Grace*, 46

CHAPTER EIGHT

Developing a Foundational Individual Relationship with God

Introduction

We will find God's presence and love when we search for Him, in Jeremiah 29:13-14a and Zechariah 1:3. Once we've found God's presence and love, we need to individually respond to God's offer of grace. Chapter eight describes four individual foundational responses to God's offer of grace. Chapter nine describes six additional individual responses to God's offer of grace that build on our foundational responses to God. Chapter ten describes our need to respond to God's offer of grace in community.

In chapter eight, I examine at least four ways to individually respond to God's presence and love in order to develop and sustain a foundational, positive, loving, personal relationship with God. Our responses to God's offer of grace will bring the hidden treasures that Jesus came to give us in John 10:10b "I came that they may have life, and have it abundantly." The four foundational ways that I examine to individually respond to God's offer of grace include: <u>First</u>, responding through our faith, <u>Second</u>, responding through our trust, <u>Third</u>, responding through our hope, and <u>Fourth</u>, responding through our love.

Responding to God's Presence and Love through Our Faith

Faith is the starting point for developing a positive, loving, personal relationship with God, because we cannot think our way to God and we cannot feel our way to God. We need to surrender to God's presence and love through our faith, trust, hope, and love in order to begin to develop our foundational relationship with God. We necessarily experience faith in our daily lives (e.g., we have faith that car drivers will stay on their side of the road.) In my opinion, faith in God is a universal phenomenon that exists in all people, because it comes from the same human dynamism that God designed into humanity in the beginning of creation, which is referenced in Acts 10:34-35. We begin our response to God's offer of grace in faith, because faith signals our acknowledgement and acceptance that we need help that cannot come from other people or other things. St. Paul assures us that God's help is present in every facet of our life, in Philippians 4:19 "And my God will fully satisfy every need of yours according to his riches in glory in Christ Jesus." It's through the gift of faith that we're able to surrender to the Absolute Mystery of God, who is the ground and the horizon of our existence, in Romans 1:17 "¹⁷For in it [faith] the righteousness of God is revealed through faith for faith; as it is written, 'The one who is righteous will live by faith.'"

Throughout the NT scriptures, Jesus was able to heal people because of their faith (e.g., Mark 5:27-34; 6:4-6; 11:20-24; 10:47-52.) How can we increase our faith in God? Mark 7:24-30 gives us an example of the relentless faith of a Syrophoenician woman, who pursued Jesus to cast a demon out of her daughter. Jesus eventually cured her daughter, because of her relentless faith. In my opinion, this gentile woman is the only person in the NT to win an argument with Jesus.

How do we bring faith into our lives? For Rahner, we're spirits in the world designed to hear the Word of God, so we need to listen to the Word of God and follow the direction that we receive from it, in Mark 9:7 "This is my Son, the Beloved; **listen to him**!" We need to listen to God, to wait for God's responses to us, to trust in God, and to obey God's commandments. When we struggle to respond to God in faith, we need to remember that our faith is imperfect and we need God's help to build a stronger faith. Jesus' apostles struggled with their faith (e.g., when a storm arose at sea, Jesus' apostles panicked and pleaded with Jesus to save them, and Jesus questioned their faith in Mark 4:35-41; Matthew 8:23-27; and Luke 8:22-25.) We need to respond to God like the father of the boy with the demon, who prayed to Jesus in Mark 9:24 "I believe; help my unbelief!" The Judeo-Christian models of faith include but are not limited to Father Abraham in Genesis 12:1-9; 22:1-14 and Mother Mary in Luke 1:38, because they were prepared to do anything that God asked them to do; we need to follow their example.

Faith is the gift that enables us to escape from the prison of self. Faith is fundamental to helping us find God's presence and love and bringing God's treasures into our lives. For Christian believers, the benefits of faith include a more abundant life today and in eternity (cf. Romans 1:18-26.) We need to continuously walk in faith, because faith is a process. We make mistakes in the process (e.g., we ask for things that we want but are not necessarily what God wants for us.) One way to build our faith is by reading and assimilating God's Word, in Hebrews 11:3 "³By faith we understand that the worlds were prepared by the word of God, so that what is seen was made from things that are not visible." The more that we're able to accept, understand, and nourish

God's Word [God's kisses] in our lives the easier it is to walk in faith.

There are countless verses in the scriptures that give us a reason to believe in God; I want to briefly examine four examples of faith in the scriptures: <u>First</u>, King David understood how much God protected him and how much he needed God. He described his faith in God in the opening verse of his most famous psalm, Psalm 23:1 "'The LORD is my shepherd, I shall not want"; <u>Second</u>, in Genesis 37–39, we learn that Jacob's son, Joseph, was sold into slavery by his brothers out of jealousy. He was taken to Egypt and sold on the slave block to Potiphar. Joseph remained a slave for thirteen years in Genesis 37:2; 41:46 but he didn't lose his faith in God. Eventually, through his faith in God, Joseph became the second most powerful man in Egypt; <u>Third</u>, in John 1:14 we're told that Jesus is full of grace and truth. We need to believe Jesus' revelations about His Father, because of what Jesus told us about His relationship with His Father, in John 14:7 "7If you know me, you will know my Father also. From now on you do know him and have seen him;" and <u>fourth</u>, in the first epistle of John we find a very compelling reason to live by faith, in 1 John 5:4 "4for whatever is born of God conquers the world. And this is the victory that conquers the world, our faith."

We find God's presence and love by responding to God in faith, because God's presence and love gives us answers to many of our questions. The peace that faith brings to us comes from a deeper, faithful, positive, loving, personal relationship with Jesus, in John 14:27 "Peace I leave with you; my peace I give to you. I do not give to you as the world gives." God wants us to show others how God works in our lives, so we need to pass our Judeo-Christian faith onto others through our example and through our unique ministries.

There are many other explanations that claim to help us understand our everyday experiences, and some of the explanations may seem more pragmatic or even more satisfying than Judeo-Christian theology (e.g., the four noble truths, Scientology, if it feels good do it.) However, for Judeo-Christian believers, our faith is based on divinely revealed truths in the Word of God. In my opinion, if faith in God is missing from our lives, then we will define our everyday experiences very differently (e.g., our transcendent experience is simply an extension of our sense experience.) Most importantly, without faith in our lives we miss out on God's hidden treasures (e.g., Matthew 6:19-34.)

In Psalm 73, the psalmist concluded that even though the mysteries of life persist, his faith in God's presence and love assures his happiness, in Psalm 73:28 "[28]But for me it is good to be near God; I have made the Lord GOD my refuge, to tell of all your works." Despite everything we may see around us (e.g., corrupt people, corrupt institutions, unmerited suffering), God's love is still present in our lives. We need to begin to develop and sustain a positive, loving, personal relationship with God through our faith, because without a relationship with God, we have little protection from "the heart-ache and the thousand natural shocks that flesh is heir to," (*Hamlet*, Act III, Scene 1, William Shakespeare)

As mentioned previously, St. Anselm [1033–1109] gave us a wonderful description of his faith in God: "For I do not seek to understand so that I may believe; but I believe so that I may understand. For I believe this also, that 'unless I believe, I shall not understand.'"[62]

Responding to God's Presence snd Love through Our Trust

Faith in God is our necessary starting point to search for answers to our many questions, but faith alone is insufficient. For Christian believers, <u>St. Peter taught us that our faith and hope in God is grounded in our trust in God,</u> in 1 Peter 1:21 "²¹'Through him [Jesus] you have come to trust in God, who raised him from the dead and gave him glory, so that your faith and hope are set on God."

We need to trust in God with all our hearts, because trust allows us to move beyond faith into a deeper,

---

62   St. Anselm, *Proslogian*, 115

positive, loving, personal relationship with God, in Proverbs 3:5-8. The psalmist was certain that we need to trust God, in Psalm 40:4 "⁴Happy are those who make the LORD their trust, who do not turn to the proud, to those who go astray after false gods." The false gods include but are not limited to power, money, envy, lust. We cannot trust the values of the world (e.g., money, power.) **St. John** Chrysostom [347-407] wrote: "It is not enough to leave Egypt, one must also travel to the Promised Land."[63] In other words, we begin our journey home to God in faith but we need to develop a deeper trust in God in order to develop a deeper personal loving relationship with Him.

We need to continually trust in God rather than trusting in a secular world that only hinders our search for the truth. Martin Buber understood our need to trust in God in our search for the truth, when he taught us "the world wants to be deceived. The truth is too complex and frightening; the taste for the truth is an acquired taste that few acquire."[64] In John's Gospel, Jesus explains why Buber's analysis is correct, in John 3:19 "¹⁹And this is the judgment, that the light [truth] has come into the world, and people loved darkness rather than light [truth] because their deeds were evil."

---

63 St. John Chrysostom, In Matthaei Evangelium, 39:4, P.G. 57:438

64 Martin Buber, *I and Thou*, 9

We need to trust that God will keep His promises to us that are described throughout the scriptures (e.g., Hebrews 13:5.) In other words, we need to bet on God, not on mammon. The more we trust that God is helping us in our everyday lives, the deeper our relationship with God will become. Jesus had a confident trust that God is who He says He is and that God will do what He says He will do, in John 12:45-46 "And whoever sees me sees him who sent me. [46]I have come as light [truth] into the world, so that everyone who believes in me should not remain in the darkness." Trust is a positive, loving, personal response from us (e.g., surrendering to God's will [Thy will be done]) and trust leads us to God's best for our life.) God's nature is to give us His best based on our individual gifts. We cannot deny that our anxiety exists, but we can turn our anxiety into trust in God, in Proverbs 1:33 "but those who listen to me will be secure and will live at ease, without dread of disaster."

We need to accept the fact that occasionally our trust in God will fail (e.g., the Israelites, who witnessed all of God's miracles that led them out of Egypt, sometimes failed to trust in God.) When the Israelite reconnaissance team returned from scouting the Promised Land, they presented a negative report about being able to defeat the existing tribes in Canaan (e.g., the enemy are giants; they're too strong, we cannot defeat this enemy.) The Israelites failed to trust in God.

Joshua and Caleb trusted in God no matter the cost, and they warned the Israelites not to rebel against God regarding going into Canaan, which led some Israelites to wanting to stone them, in Numbers 13–14. In the end, Joshua and Caleb lived to go into the Promised Land, unlike their fellow Israelites who rebelled against God.

It's possible to ignore God's presence and love in our lives by dismissing God in our lives (e.g., my life is good; I don't need God.) However, in my experience, human beings need to trust in something, so the question is never whether we believe and trust in something. The question is, what do we believe and trust in (e.g., God, ourselves, our parents, the Church, the empirical sciences of post-modernity, the omniscient state.) This leads me to Proverbs 3:5 "⁵Trust in the LORD with all your heart, and do not rely on your own insight." We need to trust that when our prayers are not answered, it's because God wants something better for us. In my opinion, Psalm 23 is the most famous biblical example of trusting in God (e.g., **Psalm 23:1** "The Lord is my shepherd, I shall not want.") Psalm 23 describes the trust that an individual [or a community] needs to have in their divine shepherd, and throughout Psalm 23's imagery, the psalmist [King David] described finding peace of mind, because of his unrelenting faith and trust in God.

Responding to God's Presence and Love through Our Hope

Hope is the powerful, optimistic desire for something good to happen. In my opinion, the degree of hope that we have in God is proportional to the degree of faith and trust that we have in God, that is, the more we believe and trust in God the deeper our hope is that God will fulfill His promises. By contrast, despair is the absence of hope, but God is the cure for despair and hopelessness. What should we hope for? For Judeo-Christian believers, our hope is rooted in our belief that God loves us and that we're never alone, because God will never abandon His children, in Hebrews 13:5 "I will never leave you or forsake you." In the Synoptic Gospels, Jesus' ministry is shaped by His hope in the coming kingdom [reign] of God, in Mark 1:15 "The time is fulfilled, and the kingdom of God has come near; repent, and believe in the good news." Throughout the Synoptic Gospels, Jesus described His hope in the coming of God's kingdom [reign.] In Matthew 6:33, Jesus taught us His most important hope for us, which is obtaining a better righteousness that will lead us to the kingdom [reign] of God.

The stronger our desire or need, the more we hold onto our hope. In 1 Samuel 1:1-18, Hannah prayed for a son but her prayers went unanswered for a long period of time. Still, Hannah never gave up her hope of having a son and eventually her prayers were answered. Hannah thanked and praised God in her beautiful hymn to God in 1 Samuel 2:1-10. St. Paul understood hope as something unseen, in Romans 8:24 "[24]For who hopes for what is seen?" St. Paul described the many hardships in his ministry in 2 Corinthians 11:24-28 and he assured us that through all his hardships he always found hope and strength in Jesus, in Philippians 4:13 "[13]I can do all things through him [Jesus] who strengthens me." How can we strengthen our hope in God? Paul answered that question in Romans 15:4 "For whatever was written in earlier times was written for our instruction, so that by steadfastness and encouragement of the scriptures we might have hope."

The objects of our hope could be many things, but the source of our hope should always be God, because hope is God's gift that sustains purpose in our lives. For Judeo-Christian believers, our hope is in God (e.g., we're saved by the grace and the mercy of God, in Psalms 39:7 "[7]My hope is in you [God.]") We're all hopelessly imprisoned in sin until we decide to place our hope in God's mercy. For Judeo-Christian believers, our feelings of hopelessness and despair can be assuaged by believing and trusting in God, in Hebrews 13:5; Genesis 28:15; and Joshua 1:5.

For William Lynch SJ, "Hope is the very heart and center of a human being."[65] We need to respond to God's presence and love in hope, because hope grounds our humanity. Through the gift of hope, we acknowledge God's design for our lives, because our Judeo-Christian hope is based on trusting in God's wisdom and power rather than trusting in our own wisdom and power (e.g., Proverbs 3:5-7; Psalm 32:8), or worse, trusting in the wisdom and power of the secular world. For Lynch, we need to avoid the contrary indicators to hope (e.g., hopelessness and despair); but at the same time, we need to maintain realistic expectations in our human interactions (e.g., we cannot trust everyone we meet, and we cannot become perfect in this life.) Throughout his book *Images of Hope*, Lynch defined three major realities that are rooted in the gift of hope: First, hope is the very heart of every human being; Second, hopelessness characterizes all forms of mental illness; and Third, imagination can be a healer of the hopeless, because what we imagine has not yet happened. The more we expect something in the future the less we tend to suffer in the present. Our best hope is relying on God's truth.[66]

In the movie, *The Ten Commandments*, Edward G. Robinson described the Israelite God to the Egyptian

---

65 William F Lynch SJ, *Images of Hope*, 9

66 William F. Lynch SJ, *Images of Hope*, 196

authorities as, "the hope of the hopeless." Nevertheless, the Israelites remained hopeful in their God and they were rewarded. On the road to Emmaus, two disciples walked with Jesus but they did not recognize Him, because they felt hopeless, because of the death of the Messiah, in Luke 24:21 "[21]But we had hoped that he was the one to redeem Israel." Even though people may try to steal our hope, Christian believers never need to feel hopeless. The hope of Christians is for eternal union with God's presence and love and the basis for Christian hope is our belief that Jesus was raised from the dead and that we will be raised from the dead to share eternal life with God, in John 17:3.

For Otto Hentz SJ, hope is the engine that drives the theological gifts, "Hope moves us to faith and then, finding its support in faith, hope moves us to love. Hope moves us to love and love leads to deeper faith. Hoping is the fundamental act out of which faith and love arise, and they in turn foster its growing power. Hope, then, is the central dynamic of the human spirit, its power to reach."[67] God must always be our hope, because we have endless frailties; so, I repeat my previous thoughts on our need to increase our faith, trust, and dependence on God in order to increase our hope in God's promises throughout the scriptures (e.g., Isaiah 60:19-22; 1 Peter 1:21; Revelation 7:16-17; 21:3-4.)

---

[67] Otto Hentz SJ, *The Hope of the Christian*, 9

Responding to God's Presence and Love through Our Love

We need to respond to God's presence and love by sharing our own capacity to love, because love brings things into existence. Without love nothing at all would exist. We cannot force anyone to love us, because love comes from someone's freedom. Similarly, God cannot force us to love Him; we love God through our freedom to love. However, we can always be certain of God's steadfast love and faithfulness to us (e.g., Psalms. 25:10; 40:11; 57:3; 86:15; 89:14.) Love is the most positive emotion in our lives and it's built on our faith, trust, and hope. Love accepts, affirms, and approves whomever and whatever it loves, and reason alone can never fully account for the choice and the intensity of either human love or divine love. In 1964, Peter and Gordon recorded a popular song and their lyrics told us that they couldn't stay in a world without love. As previously discussed, the offer of God's grace [God's presence and love] permeates God's theocentric world; so, we don't have to stay in a world without love. Indeed, the greater our faith, trust, and hope in God the greater our ability to love God, self, and others.

The scriptures are replete with examples of God's love for us (e.g., Exodus 15:13 "[13]In your steadfast love you led the people whom you redeemed; you guided them by your strength to your holy abode.") The scriptures are also replete with God's directions to us concerning our need to love God and others (e.g., John 13:34-35 "³⁴I give you a new commandment, that you love one another. Just as I have loved you, you also should love one another. ³⁵By this everyone will know that you are my disciples, if you have love for one another."

The NT tells us that God is love in 1 John 4:8, 16, and God's love constitutes the essence of His creative work in Genesis 12:1ff; John 1:1-5, 9-18; Hebrews 1:1-3; and Colossians 1:15-20 and God's redemptive work in Isaiah 40–55 and John 3:16-17. In the first epistle of John, we're told that we're able to love because we were first loved, in 1 John 4:19-20 "¹⁹We love because he first loved us. ²⁰Those who say, 'I love God,' and hate their brothers or sisters, are liars; for those who do not love a brother or sister whom they have seen, cannot love God whom they have not seen."

We're called to love God, self, and others, and God's gift of the indwelling Spirit gives us the greatest capacity to love and to be loved. Luke's beautiful story about the Prodigal Son in Luke 15:11-32 dramatically illustrates that one of his sons' desire for erotic love could not wait but his father's genuine love had the patience to wait. In other words, <u>God is patiently waiting for us to search for Him,</u> in Jeremiah 29:13-14a and Zechariah 1:3. Genuine love is joyful, generous, forgiving, and it seeks the benefit of the other. The father of the prodigal son waited for and celebrated his son's return, and our Father will wait for and celebrate our return home.

How does love help us in a practical sense in our daily lives? Love helps us to trust and thank God in all of life's circumstances, to wait patiently for God's answers to our prayers, to forgive others, to serve God and others joyfully, to be generous in sharing our gifts, and to become the person we're intended to become "a self-for-others." We're given the gift of love and we need to use our freedom to love God, self, and others. In the Catechism of the Catholic Church, we're taught that "Love is itself the fulfillment of all our works. There is the goal; that is why we run; we run towards it, and once we reach it, in it we shall find rest."[68]

God's love for us is very clear in Isaiah's fourth suffering servant song, Isaiah 52:13–53:12. I want to focus on a specific part of Second Isaiah's description of the suffering servant in his fourth suffering servant song in Isaiah 53:2b-3 "[2b]he had no form or majesty that we should look at him, nothing in his appearance that we should desire him. [3]He was despised and rejected by others; a man of suffering and acquainted with infirmity; and as one from whom others hide their faces he was despised, and we held him of no account." In my opinion, on the cross, Jesus did have a form and a

---

68 "Catechism of the Catholic Church," article 1829

majesty; it was the form and majesty of love. In contrast to Rahner's theological anthropology, which studies God starting from humanity, Isaiah 53:2b-3 provides an opportunity to study God starting from divinity, that is, starting from the form and majesty and love of God's vicarious suffering servant. We show our love for God and others by the lives we lead and the ministries we pursue. We all need to belong, and love provides an important way to show each other that we belong. Responding to God with love is a powerful way to find His presence and love in our lives. As previously stated, I agree with C. S. Lewis' answer to his rhetorical question/answer in the movie *Shadowlands*: what does God want from us? God wants us: "to love, to be loved, and to grow up." We should always remember where our capacity to love comes from, in 1 John 4:19 "We love because he first loved us." And we should always remember that God's mercy comes from His unwavering steadfast love for us.

CHAPTER NINE

Developing a Deeper Individual Relationship with God

Introduction

Having established a foundational relationship with God in faith, trust, hope, and love, we're ready to further develop our relationship with God and find a better righteousness. In my experience, I've found at least six additional ways to respond to God's offer of grace [God's presence and love] in order to develop, nurture, and sustain a deeper personal relationship with God: <u>First</u>, through our prayers, <u>Second</u>, through our obedience to God, <u>Third</u>, through our discipleship, <u>Fourth</u>, through reading and studying the Word of God, <u>Fifth</u>, through becoming a self-for-others, and <u>Sixth</u>, through our joy and thanksgiving.

Responding to God's Presence and Love through Our Prayers

Praying is an act of faith that expresses at least three things that we believe: <u>First</u>, we believe that God exists; <u>Second</u>, we believe that we need God's help; and <u>Third</u>, we believe that we're able to communicate with God. Why do we pray to God? We pray to God because our prayers allow us to have a privileged conversation with Him, who unconditionally loves us. In the Gospels, Jesus often prayed to His Father (e.g., Luke 6:12 "¹²Now during those days he went out to the mountain to pray; and he spent the night in prayer to God.) For Judeo-Christian believers, we need to pray to God in faith, trust, hope, and love.

God has guided Judeo-Christian believers in prayer for thousands of years. Our prayers bring us closer to God's presence and love and they acknowledge that we need to talk with God in order to communicate our daily needs for ourselves and others. More importantly, we need to listen to God. The psalmist prayed to God in his loneliness and despair, in Psalm 102:1-3 "¹Hear my prayer, O LORD; let my cry come to you. ²Do not hide your face from me in the day of my distress. Incline your ear to me; answer me speedily in the day when I call. ³For my days pass away like smoke, and my bones burn like a furnace."

If we don't pray to God, that is, if we don't communicate with God, then we're not going to have a close personal relationship with Him. For Christian believers, God doesn't force us into a positive, loving, personal relationship with Him, but we're oriented into a relationship with God through the Holy Spirit that indwells us. However, we cannot limit our prayers to an SOS call to God whenever we're in trouble, because God is not our personal SOS answering service. We need to patiently pray to God and patiently trust that God will answer our prayers, in Isaiah 64:4 "⁴From ages past no one has heard, no ear has perceived, no eye has seen any God besides you, who works for those who wait for him." Most importantly, when we're waiting for an answer to our prayers, <u>we can only know if God is communicating with us if we're listening to God</u>. Prayer will strengthen our individual faith, trust, hope, and love for God and it can lead us into God's work (e.g., praying for others, helping others.)

There are several books that describe various elements of praying to God, but I want to focus on just five elements of praying to Him: <u>First</u>, Jesus taught us why we need to pray; <u>Second</u>, the psalmists gave us magnificent prayers to pray to God; <u>Third</u>, Catholics can pray to God in at least six ways; <u>Fourth</u>, Huns Urs von Balthasar SJ, describes the reality of prayer in our lives; and <u>Fifth</u>, God always answers our prayers but not necessarily in the way we want or in the timeframe we want.

First, Jesus taught us why we need to pray, in John 15:5 "⁵I am the vine, you are the branches. Those who abide in me and I in them bear much fruit, because apart from me you can do nothing." In my opinion, there are three fundamental components to responding to God in prayer: First, we need to begin our prayers by thanking God for all our blessings and gifts; Second, we need to enter into a dialogue with God – not a monologue; and Third, we need to trust that God will answer our prayers in His own way and in His own time (e.g., the psalmist assured us that we need to wait for God to respond to our prayers, in Psalm 130:5-6 "⁵I wait for the LORD, my soul waits, and in his word I hope; ⁶my soul waits for the Lord more than those who watch for the morning, more than those who watch for the morning.") And the Gospels resonate with the psalmist's words in Matthew 17:5 "⁵This is my Son, the Beloved; with him I am well pleased; listen to him!"

Second, the psalmists give us magnificent prayers to pray to God, which makes the psalms a treasure for all Judeo-Christian believers. For example, in Psalm 62 we read a hymn of trust in God, because the psalmist feels that he's been forsaken and that he's being persecuted by his former friends, who have become influential enemies. The psalmist's adversaries have attacked him so much that he's worn down and in danger of succumbing to their pressure, as he describes his central response to God in Psalm 62:5-6 "⁵For God alone my soul waits in silence, for my hope is from him. ⁶He alone is my rock [my protection] and my salvation [my deliverance], my fortress [my home]; I shall not be shaken." The psalmist trusts in God's protection, because he knows that humans cannot help him. The psalmist goes further in Psalm 62:7 "⁷On God rests my deliverance and my honor; my mighty rock, <u>my refuge is in God</u>." The psalmist's trust in God gives him a new source of strength, safety, and peace in his life. Our faith, trust, hope, and love brought into our prayers to God will bring us the same assurance that the psalmist felt.

<u>Third, Catholics can pray to God in at least six ways</u>: <u>First</u>, we can pray directly to God the Father in our own words or through the beautiful prayers in the scriptures (e.g., in the Psalms and in the Gospels); <u>Second</u>, when Jesus' disciples asked Him to teach them how to pray, Jesus taught them [and us] to pray the "Our Father" in Luke 11:1-4 and Matthew 6:5-14; <u>Third</u>, we can pray directly to Jesus in John 15:7 "⁷If you abide in me, and my words abide in you, ask for whatever you wish, and it will be done for you;" <u>Fourth</u>, many Catholics pray to Jesus through Mother Mary, as the Marist Brothers say: "To Jesus through Mary", because it was through Mary's

humility and selflessness that Jesus came into the world, in Luke 1:38); <u>Fifth</u>, many Catholics pray to Catholic saints (e.g., to their patron saint or to a chosen saint like St. Jude, the patron saint of lost causes.) The idea of praying to the saints is addressed in the Catechism of the Catholic Church where we're told: "The witnesses who have preceded us into the kingdom, especially, those whom the Church recognizes as saints, share in the living tradition of prayer by the example of their lives;"[69] and <u>Sixth</u>, all Judeo-Christian believers need to pray to God in community (e.g., Jesus' apostles and disciples were gathered in community in prayer after Jesus was murdered, in Acts 1:14.) Therefore, we need to gather in community prayer (e.g., worshipping God in the weekly Mass, on Holy Days, or on special occasions such as celebrating the sacraments of Baptism or Marriage.) Jesus assured us that He would be present anywhere two or three were gathered in His name, in Matthew 18:20.

<u>Fourth, Huns Urs von Balthasar SJ describes the reality of prayer in our lives</u> in his excellent book called *Prayer*: "The kingdom [reign] of God is eternally real not temporally real; so, we need to surrender to the reality of the eternal reign of God. We do not build the kingdom [reign] of God on earth by our own efforts (however assisted by grace); the most we can do, through genuine

---

[69] "Catechism of the Catholic Church," article 2683

prayer, is to make as much room as possible, in ourselves and in the world, for the kingdom [reign] of God, so that its energies can go to work."[70] St. Paul taught the early church community in Thessalonica [and us] how to approach Christian life in 1 Thessalonians 5:17 "[17]<u>pray without ceasing</u>." And St. Paul's teaching still resonates today, "<u>pray without ceasing</u>."

<u>Fifth, God always answers our prayers</u> but not necessarily in the timeframe that we want and not necessarily with the answers that we want. For Christian believers, Jesus gave us an advocate, the Holy Spirit, who abides in our deepest consciousness. The job of the Holy Spirit of God, our Advocate, is to guide us and help us, in Romans 8:26-27. Our prayers should always resonate with Jesus' prayerful answer to His Father in Mark 14:36; Matthew 26:39, 42; John 12:27; and Luke 22:42 "not my will but yours be done."

Responding to God's Presence and Love through Our Obedience

We continue to develop our positive, loving, personal relationship with God through our obedience to God, because we will more fully experience God's presence and love in our lives when we stop putting other things in front of God, in Exodus 20:2-3 "[2]I am the LORD your

---

[70] Hans Urs von Balthasar SJ, *Prayer*, 105

God, who brought you out of the land of Egypt, out of the house of slavery; ³you shall have no other gods before me." We need to keep God first in our lives by praying to God, by listening to God, and by being obedient to God (e.g., in our seeing, in our hearing, in our reading, and especially, in the way we treat our sisters and brothers.) Jesus responded to His Father in obedience in Luke 22:42 "⁴²Father, if you are willing, remove this cup from me; yet, not my will but yours be done." We need to follow Jesus' example of obedience to God and share Jesus' confidence in His Father in John 8:29 "²⁹And the one who sent me is with me; he has not left me alone, for I always do what is pleasing to him." God wants the best things for us. Today, we're blessed with God's handbook of instructions in the scriptures, which is designed to help us understand and respond to God's presence and love in our daily lives (e.g., Genesis 22:1-19; John 14:15-24; Ephesians 6:1-3.) In my opinion, Jesus' most pragmatic guidance on obedience is found in John 14:15 "¹⁵If you love me, you will keep [obey] my commandments." We need to remember that God doesn't ask us to do anything that we're not capable of doing! And God does not tempt us beyond our ability to resist the temptation, in 1 Corinthians 10:13!

We need to remember that God is our eternally loving Father. We teach young children to obey us because we have a better idea than they do of what's best for them.

Similarly, Father God has a better idea of what's best for us than we do. Most parents try to teach their kids to make good choices in order to avoid problems, in Luke 11:11-13 "[11]Is there anyone among you who, if your child asks for a fish, will give a snake instead of a fish? [12]Or if the child asks for an egg, will give a scorpion? [13]If you then, who are evil, know how to give good gifts to your children, how much more will the heavenly Father give the Holy Spirit to those who ask him!"

The book of Proverbs begins with ten lectures that a father gives to his son to teach him how to make morally correct choices, in Proverbs 1:8–7:27. I want to briefly examine the opening verses of the first lecture, in Proverbs 1:8-9 "[8]Hear, my child, your father's instruction, and do not reject your mother's teaching; [9]for they are a fair garland for your head, and pendants for your neck." Throughout the parent's teaching (e.g., in the first lecture), the young boy is shown two alternatives: First, he can follow the truth and honor his mother and father or Second, he can follow the deceivers and be punished. Unfortunately, boys and girls quickly learn that deceivers are not always punished nor are the righteous always rewarded, which challenges our instruction to our children and similarly, God's instruction to us. At least two OT wisdom books try to clarify the reward-punishment theological doctrine by challenging its assumptions (e.g., the books of Job and

Ecclesiastes.) Nevertheless, most parents continue to teach their children to do what's best for them in the long run and similarly, that's what God's instructions to us in the scriptures [God's teaching] are designed to accomplish.

Jesus isn't asking us to change our careers. He is asking us to change our perspective and our orientation (e.g., in some way become a self-for-others in order to participate in God's presence and love more fully.) In John's Gospel, Jesus instructed us how to walk through our daily lives, in John 8:12 "[12]Again Jesus spoke to them, saying, 'I am the light [truth] of the world. Whoever follows me will never walk-in darkness but will have the light of life.'" We're called to experience God's glory and share it with others in 2 Corinthians 4:6. We're not all called or equipped to be evangelists but we're all called to be obedient to God's commandments and in some way serve others through our example and through our unique gifts and ministries, because that's how we become fully human, in Mark 12:28-34; Matthew 22:34-40; and Luke 10:25-28.

Responding to God's Presence and Love through Our Discipleship

We continue to develop our positive, loving, personal relationship with God through our discipleship. Our prayers and our obedience to God help us to understand that God didn't give us our gifts, talents, virtues, and even our expertise for ourselves alone. We need to become an extension of God on earth (e.g., by bearing fruit through our various ministries, because we belong to God not to ourselves, in Matthew 7:20 "²⁰Thus you will know them by their fruits.") Jesus described certain conditions and promises that occur, when we become His disciples, in Luke 17:33 "³³Those who try to make their life secure will lose it, but those who lose their life will keep it."

However, discipleship may be very costly to us. So, I want to describe three examples of costly discipleship: <u>First</u>, in active missionary work; <u>Second</u>, in daily witnessing to God; and <u>Third</u>, in costly grace. <u>First</u>, missionary work in all four Gospels is not an abstract idea (e.g., one of the costs of discipleship for Jesus' apostles was leaving everything to follow Jesus, in Mark 1:18; Matthew 4:19; Luke 5:11; John 1:35-42.) In Matthew and Luke's Gospel, the apostle's missionary work is described in the mission of the Twelve, in Matthew 10:5-15 and Luke 9:1-6 and again in the mission of the Seventy in Luke 10:1ff. Missionary work is extended to all of Jesus' disciples in the book of Acts, in Acts 1:8 "⁸But you will receive power when the Holy Spirit has come upon you; and you will be my witnesses in Jerusalem, in all Judea and Samaria, and to the ends of the earth.") Missionary work is also extended to all of Jesus' disciples in Matthew's Gospel, in Matthew 28:19-20 and John's Gospel, in John 20:21.

Second, most of us are not equipped to be missionaries; however, Christian believers are called to be witnesses to God through their example, through their discipleship, and through their service to others (e.g., we need to develop our own unique ministry, which can be part time or full time, but somehow, we need to become a self-for-others.) We can certainly find many voids in the world which provide the opportunities to apply our unique gifts, talents, and expertise (e.g., visiting a sick relative, helping a relative or a neighbor with their errands, teaching scriptures.)

Third, Dietrich Bonhoeffer taught us that grace can be costly or cheap. Bonhoeffer saw the danger to western civilization before Hitler's nationalism moved God completely out of the public square. Bonhoeffer taught us that "costly grace" outwardly condemns sin. He taught us that cheap grace operates in the secular world, especially when bad situations become worse, which is primarily caused by apathy or fear. Our discipleship cannot be based on cheap grace. The costs to Bonhoeffer for defying NAZI Germany included losing his prestigious teaching position, his imprisonment, and eventually losing his life. We hopefully won't be called to pay the price that Bonhoeffer paid, but we are called to stand our ground in defense of God and in defense of all the threats to our religious beliefs regardless of the cost to us (e.g., our safety, our jobs, and even our lives.) This was Jesus' message to Paul in Acts 26:16 "[16]But get up and stand on your feet; for I have appeared to you for this purpose, to appoint you to serve and testify to the things in which you have seen me and to those in which I will appear to you." We need to be able to explain and defend the God that we believe in to other people! St. Peter also told us to stand our ground in defense of our faith, in 1 Peter 3:15 "Always be ready to make your defense to anyone who demands from you an accounting for the hope that is in you." Jesus taught us a very positive way to understand costly grace, in Matthew 13:45 "[45]Again, the kingdom of heaven is like a merchant in search of fine pearls; [46]on finding one pearl of great value, he went and sold all that he had and bought it." In other words, nothing was more important to the merchant than the pearl of great value and nothing was more important to Jesus in Matthew 6:33 than teaching us to obtain a better righteousness that will lead to our fulfillment in the kingdom [reign] of God.

Responding to God's Presence and Love through Reading and Studying the Word of God

Throughout my book I have quoted and referenced many verses from scriptures, because the Word of God provides a thematic way to find God's presence and love in our daily lives. The more we pray to God, the more we are obedient to God, and the more we try to pass on God's Word in our discipleship (e.g., by being an example of Jesus), the better equipped we become to read, study, and assimilate the Word of God.

What's the benefit of reading and studying the scriptures? Reading and studying the Word of God gives us the opportunity to develop a deeper, positive, loving, personal relationship with God, because the scriptures provide a blueprint that guides us to a better righteousness. Scriptures teach us what God has to say about how we should live our daily lives. Scriptures comfort us, guide us, inspire us, awe us, delight us, and they give us hope (e.g., for resurrection into the eternal kingdom [reign] of God.) The scriptures give us the opportunity to encounter God's presence and love in our hearts (e.g., Deuteronomy 8:3 "³He humbled you by letting you hunger, then by feeding you with manna, with which neither you nor your ancestors were acquainted, in order to make you understand that <u>one does not live by bread alone, but by every word that comes from the mouth of the LORD</u>.") Isaiah beautifully described the power of God's Word in Isaiah 55:10-11 "¹⁰For as the rain and the snow come down from heaven and do not return there until they have watered the earth, making it bring forth and sprout, giving seed to the sower and bread to the eater, [11]so shall my word be that goes out from my mouth; it shall not return to me empty, but it shall accomplish that which I purpose and succeed in the thing for which I sent it."

The scriptures provide at least three ways to know God's presence and love: <u>First</u>, through the thirty-nine books of the OT; <u>Second,</u> through the fourteen books of the Apocrypha [Intertestamental literature or IT]; and <u>Third,</u> through the twenty-seven books of the NT. All eighty books of the Bible give us a deeper more personal understanding of God's presence and love in our daily lives. In my opinion, the fundamental point of all eighty books of scriptures is to bring us to an encounter with God's presence and love [God's amazing grace.]

<u>First, finding God's presence and love in the thirty-nine books of the OT literature can be accomplished in several ways</u> (e.g., think of the thirty-nine books of the OT being organized into three concentric circles.) The innermost circle contains the first five books of the Bible [Genesis, Exodus, Leviticus, Numbers, and Deuteronomy]; these books are called the Torah or the Pentateuch. The middle circle contains the fifteen prophets for Jewish believers, which help us to understand the Torah. The outer circle contains the remaining nineteen books of the OT called the writings (e.g., the book of Psalms.) The writings help us to understand the prophets and the Torah.

Another way to understand the thirty-nine books of OT literature is to study their many different genres. For example, studying <u>historical literature</u> includes studying primordial, patriarchal, and exodus history in the first five books of the OT; Deuteronomist history, which includes the book of Deuteronomy and the next six books of the OT [Joshua, Judges, 1 & 2 Samuel and 1 & 2 Kings] and additional historical books (e.g., the books of the Chronicler, Ezra, Nehemiah); studying <u>prophetic literature</u> (e.g., the three major prophets Isaiah, Jeremiah, and Ezekiel and the twelve minor prophets); studying <u>wisdom literature</u> (e.g., the books of Proverbs, Job, Ecclesiastes, and the Song of Songs); and studying <u>apocalyptic literature</u> (e.g., Isaiah 24–27.) OT literature is certain of God's steadfast faithfulness, mercy, and love for His people even in times of terrible hardship (e.g., Psalm 136 and Lamentations 3:22-23 "²²The steadfast love of the LORD never ceases, his mercies never come to an end; "²³they are new every morning; <u>great is your faithfulness</u>.")

For some commentators, the song of songs [the canticle of canticles], describes God's presence and love for humanity allegorically in Canticles 1:2 "²Let him kiss me with the kisses of his mouth! For your love is better than wine." For Larry Lyke, God's allegorical kissing in Canticles 1:2 is associated with Moses receiving the Torah [the Pentateuch.][71] I would extend Lyke's

---

[71] Larry L. Lyke, *I Will Espouse You Forever*, 71-73

allegorical kissing in Canticles 1:2 to the entire eighty books of the Bible, because I believe that God's kisses are found in all eighty books of the scriptures (e.g., Isaiah 55:10-11.) The psalmist was confident of God's kisses, faithfulness, and love for him in Psalm 143:1-2, 9 "¹Hear my prayer, O LORD; give ear to my supplications in your faithfulness; <u>answer me in your righteousness</u>. ²Do not enter judgment with your servant, for <u>no one living is righteous before you</u>... ⁹Save me, O LORD, from my enemies; I have fled to you for refuge."

<u>Second, finding God's presence and love in IT literature</u> begins by understanding that there are fourteen books of intertestamental literature generally called the books of the Apocrypha. These fourteen books are not canonical for Jewish believers and most Protestant believers; however, these fourteen books are canonical for some Christian denominations and seven of the fourteen books of the Apocrypha are considered deuterocanonical for Roman Catholics. I'm a Roman Catholic, so I focus on the seven books of IT that are deuterocanonical for Catholics including the books of Tobit, Judith, the book of Wisdom [also called the Wisdom of Solomon], the book of Sirach [also called the book of Ecclesiasticus], Baruch, and 1 & 2 Maccabees. The books of the Apocrypha include many wonderful narratives, but I'll just briefly mention a few. In the book of Judith, Judith saves Israel through her faith

and trust in God and through her feminine wiles. God created wisdom (e.g., Proverbs 8:22-31) and God told us where to find wisdom in Job 28:1-28. These stories are retold in the book of Sirach in Sirach 24:1-22 and the book of Wisdom in Wisdom 6:12-25.

Third, finding God's presence and love in the twenty-seven books of NT scriptures is easy for Christian believers, because of Jesus' gift of an advocate [the Holy Spirit indwelling in us], in John 14:16-17; 14:25-26; 16:7, who is immanently present to us and who helps us to read and study the scriptures. For Christian believers, Jesus is the fullest revelation of God's presence and love, in John 1:1-5, 14; Matthew 1:23; Luke 1:35; and Galatians 4:4-5. The best reason to study the NT comes from Jesus' teaching on how to find eternal life in John 17:3 "And this is eternal life, that they may know you, the only true God, and Jesus Christ whom you have sent." In NT scriptures, the key to obtaining eternal life is to know the only true God and Jesus Christ whom God sent. However, for Christian believers, to truly understand and enjoy the abundant richness of NT scriptures, we need to better understand who Jesus is and what Jesus did. Jesus taught His apostles the way to find God in John 14:6a "⁶ᵃJesus said to him, 'I am the way, and the truth, and the life.'" Jesus is the way to the Father but God the Father is the destination. Studying Jesus' life, ministry, death, resurrection, and ascension back to His Father is the easiest way to understand the transcendent Absolute Mystery of God, because Jesus tells us in John 14:7 "*7*<u>If you know me, you will know my Father also</u>. From now on you do know him and have seen him."

What is the best way to know Jesus? For Tom Stegman SJ, the Gospels provide a privileged way to know Jesus from His teaching.[72] The four Gospels tell us who Jesus is and what Jesus did; so, one way to begin to study the NT is to find our own answer to two questions about Jesus: <u>First</u>, "who do you say I am" and <u>Second</u>, "what do you say I do?" In the Synoptic Gospels, Jesus asked His apostles in Matthew 16:15 "He said to them, '<u>But who do you say that I am?</u>'" I begin with a general answer to these questions and then I provide my opinion of how each Gospel evangelist answered these questions. However, each Christian believer has to answer these two questions for themselves, because God's presence and love is found in our own individual answers to these questions.

<u>The most general answer to the question: "who do you say I am</u>" can be discerned by examining the Christological titles that each Gospel evangelist assigns to Jesus (e.g., all four Gospel evangelists use the same four Christological titles for Jesus: Jesus is the Messiah [the Christ], Jesus is Lord, Jesus is the Son of God,

---

[72] Thomas D. Stegman SJ, *Opening the Door of Faith*, 4

and Jesus is the Son of Man.) Each Gospel evangelist may then add their own unique Christological titles to Jesus (e.g., John's Gospel adds at least three unique Christological titles for Jesus: Jesus is the Word of God, Jesus is the Lamb of God, and Jesus is the Good Shepherd.)

<u>The most general answer to the question: "what do you say I do" is "Savior.</u>" The NT teaches us that out of love for humanity, God took the initiative to make His presence and love more accessible to us through Jesus' revelations (e.g., John 3:16-17; 12:47-50.) We need to understand God's presence and love in our lives because we cannot save ourselves, in Psalm 80:19 "[19]Restore us, O Lord God of hosts; let your face shine, that we may be saved." We need to rely on God's grace and mercy in James 2:13 in order to be saved. Christian believers must remember that they need to accept Jesus as both Lord and Savior. Most Christians have an easy time accepting Jesus as Savior but we must also accept Jesus as Lord (e.g., by loving and worshipping Jesus, by being obedient to Jesus' teaching, and by becoming a self-for-others.)

<u>Mark's Gospel answers the question: "who do you say I am"</u> in the first verse of his Gospel, in Mark 1:1 "'The beginning of the good news of <u>Jesus Christ, the Son of God.</u>" The leitmotif in Mark's Gospel is the messianic secret, that is, Jesus rejected the title

"Messiah" because His disciples, the Jewish people, and the Jewish leaders did not understand what the title "Messiah" meant. Later in Mark's Gospel, Jesus asked His apostles who they thought He was. Peter, speaking for all the apostles, responded in Mark 8:29 "You are the Messiah." The Greek translation of Messiah is **Khristós, which was a**nglicized to Christ and this Christological title [Jesus, the Christ] became the normative answer to the question: who do you say I am? Ironically, Mark's other Christological title for Jesus in his opening verse, "the Son of God," is a more accurate answer to the question "who do you say I am?"

Mark's Gospel answers the question: "what do you say I do" in two ways: First, in Mark 1:38, Jesus tells His disciples that He came into the world to reveal and proclaim the good news of His Father and Second, Mark explains what Jesus is doing through his literary device of corrective Christology. Jesus predicted His passion, death, and resurrection three times in Mark's Gospel, in Mark 8:31–9:1; 9:30-32; 10:32-34, and each time His apostles misunderstood him, which allowed Jesus to correct their misunderstanding of who He is and what He is doing. Jesus' passion predictions and His passion narrative describe what Jesus did in His ministry (e.g., Jesus suffered, died, was buried, was resurrected, and ascended to eternal glory at the right hand of His Father.) Mark and Matthew's Gospels emphasize that

Jesus is the actualization of Isaiah's suffering servant, because Jesus suffered a vicarious suffering servant's death in Mark 10:45 "⁴⁵For the Son of Man came not to be served but to serve, and to give his life a ransom for many."

Matthew's Gospel answers the question: "who do you say I am" by describing Jesus as a wisdom teacher. In Matthew's Gospel, Jesus knew His Father, the highest form of Wisdom; so, Jesus is the wisdom of God. For Dunn, in the Sermon on the Mount in Matthew 5–7, Matthew describes the first explicit Wisdom Christology: "Wisdom never became more than a personification of God's own activity... Only Matthew moves beyond this to embrace explicit Wisdom Christology (Jesus = Wisdom) – and he does this by careful but obvious deliberate redaction of his Q source."[73]

Matthew's Gospel answers the question: "what do you say I do" through the leitmotif in Matthew's Gospel, that is, Jesus is the fulfillment of OT prophecies. Matthew's Gospel begins by emphasizing the purpose of Jesus' birth in Matthew 1:22-23 "²²All this took place to fulfill what had been spoken by the Lord through the prophet: ²³'Look, the virgin shall conceive and bear a son, and they shall name him Emmanuel,' which means, 'God is with us.'" Matthew's Gospel uses the word fulfill

---

[73] James D. G. Dunn, *Christology in the Making*, 210

eight times, in Matthew 1:22-23; 2:14-15; 3:13-15; 5:17; 8:17; 12:17-21; 13:35; 21:4-5; the word <u>fulfilled</u> <u>explicitly</u> six times, in Matthew 2:17-18; 2:23; 4:13-16; 26:54; 26:56; 27:9-10; and the word <u>fulfilled</u> <u>implicitly</u> five times, in Matthew 2:5-6; 3:3; 24:3; 26:20-21, 31. In addition to fulfilling OT prophecies, in His Sermon on the Mount in Matthew 5–7, Jesus taught us a new, comprehensive set of ethics, which are intended to help us find a better righteousness in order to enter the kingdom [reign] of God.

<u>Luke's Gospel answers the question: "who do you say I am"</u> in the beginning of his Gospel in Luke 2:29-32, when Simeon told Jesus' parents that he saw God's salvation in Jesus, who would become "³²a light for revelation to the Gentiles and for glory to your people Israel." Compared to Mark and Matthew's Jesus, Luke's Jesus appears to be a more Socratic figure, that is, the ideal Greek person (e.g., the final words on Jesus' mouth in Luke 23:46 "⁴⁶Then Jesus, crying with a loud voice, said, 'Father, into your hands I commend my spirit.' Having said this, he breathed his last.") By contrast, Mark 15:34-37 and Matthew 27:46-50 generally understand Jesus as Isaiah's suffering servant, who died utterly alone: "My God, my God, why have you forsaken me?"

<u>Luke's Gospel answers the question: "what do you say I do"</u> in the beginning of his Gospel; Jesus is the redeemer for Simeon and Anna in Luke 2:34-35 "³⁴Then

Simeon blessed them and said to his mother Mary, 'This child is destined for the falling and the rising of many in Israel, and to be a sign that will be opposed ³⁵so that the inner thoughts of many will be revealed—and a sword will pierce your own soul too...'" In my opinion, Luke's Gospel emphasizes that Jesus' brings universal salvation to humanity (e.g., Luke carefully selected the characters in Jesus' parables to include Jewish and Gentile characters, male and female characters, and young and old characters.) And Luke's Jesus taught us universally significant ethics (e.g., in the parable of the Good Samaritan in Luke 10:25-37 and in the parable of the Prodigal Son in Luke 15:11-32.)

<u>John's Gospel answers the question: "who do you say I am</u>" by telling us that Jesus is the pre-existent Word of God, who became incarnate [human], in John 1:1-5, 14 in the person of Jesus. Throughout John's Gospel, Jesus tells us that He is "God" or "I am," which resonates with Exodus 3:13-14. The letters rendered from "I AM who I AM" are the tetragrammaton of the consonants YHWH [God.] When Jesus was speaking to the Jewish people in Jerusalem, He told them who He was in John 8:58 "⁵⁸Jesus said to them, 'Very truly, I tell you, before Abraham was, <u>I am</u>.'" The Johannine Jesus emphasized God's presence and love in His very being through His "I am" sayings throughout John's Gospel, in John 10:7, 9; 10:11, 14; 11:25; 14:6; 15:1-5 (e.g., <u>I am</u> the light of the

world in John 8:12; 9:5.) At the end of John's Gospel, Jesus' apostle, Thomas, confesses who Jesus is: "My Lord and my God" (John 20:28.)

<u>John's Gospel answers the question: "what do you say I do</u>" by telling us that Jesus came into the world to reveal His Father and to testify to the truth in John 18:37 "For this I was born, and for this I came into the world, to testify to the truth." In the first epistle of John, we're told that Jesus' salvific death demonstrates God's love for humanity in a love that has no limits [an agape love], in 1 John 4:7-9.

In addition to answering the questions "Who do you say I am" and "What do you say I do," John's Gospel gives us at least two additional reasons to read and study Jesus' revelations to us: <u>First</u>, Jesus assured us that He is the best way to find God's presence and love, because He tells us that He is God in John 10:30 "³⁰The Father and I are one." And <u>Second</u>, Jesus assured us that we will have eternal life by knowing His Father and by knowing Him, in John 17:3 "³And <u>this is eternal life</u>, that they may know you, the only true God, and Jesus Christ whom you have sent."

In my opinion, answering these two questions helps us to develop and sustain a deeper, positive, loving, personal relationship with God. Our study of the NT will be greatly enhanced the more we understand Jesus, because Jesus is the bridge to God, in Luke 16:19-26 and

John 14:6-9. So, Jesus is the way to the Father, but God's presence and love is our destination. However, we need to be open to the truth about the salvific intent of the incarnation of God in the person of Jesus, the Christ, in John 3:16-17; 12:47-50.

Responding to God's Presence and Love through Becoming a Self-for-Others

In part four of my book, I have described several ways to respond to God's offer of grace in our lives in order to develop and sustain a deeper, positive, loving, personal relationship with God, because we share in God's security and peace, in John 14:27. Now, I describe the most difficult response to God, which is transitioning from being self-centered to becoming a self-for-others.

I begin by describing Jesus' response to a lawyer who asked Him what the greatest commandment is. Jesus' response provides us with a summary of the law and the prophets in Matthew 22:36-40 "[36]'Teacher, which commandment in the law is the greatest?' [37]He said to him, 'You shall love the Lord your God with all your heart, and with all your soul, and with all your mind.' [38]This is the greatest and first commandment [39]and a second is like it: 'You shall love your neighbor as yourself.' [40]On these two commandments hang all the law and the prophets.'" The underlying OT commandments in Jesus' response are found in Deuteronomy 6:4-5 and Leviticus 19:18.

Throughout the history of Christianity, theologians and exegetes have helped to further explain Jesus' answer to the lawyer's question. In 407, St. Augustine, in a homily for Easter Saturday, told us to "Love and do what you will." St. Thomas Aquinas was more specific, because he taught us that we need to love God, self, and others. When we respond to God from a foundational relationship (e.g., faith, trust, hope, and love), we can deepen our positive, loving, personal relationship with God through our prayers, obedience, discipleship, and reading and studying the Word of God, which will help us to know and love God, self, and others. We can begin to live in God's security and peace, in John 14:27, and we begin to develop a heightened awareness of God working in us through God's Spirit. Christ is the firstborn of the children of God, and we are created to share in the image of God's Son as adopted children of God, in Romans 8:17 "if children, then heirs, heirs of God and joint heirs with Christ." Knowing and loving God and ourselves helps us to understand Jesus' second love commandment to love your neighbor as yourself, because loving our neighbor teaches us how to obtain abundant life, the fullness of humanity, and the restoration of our original design, which was God's original plan from the beginning, in Genesis 1:26a "[26]Then God said, "Let us make humankind in our image [2 Corinthians 4:4], according to our likeness [Ephesians 4:24.]"

How do we become a self-for-others? We need to be in right relationship with God and ourselves before we can think about becoming a self-for-others. The first epistle of John provides a good starting point, in 1 John 2:9-11 "*<u>9Whoever says, "I am in the light [truth]," while hating a brother or sister, is still in the darkness.</u> 10Whoever loves a brother or sister abides in the light, and in such a person there is no cause for stumbling. 11But whoever hates a brother or sister is in the darkness, walks in the darkness, and does not know the way to go, because the darkness has brought on blindness.*" St. Paul teaches us many ways to become a self-for-others, in Romans 12:6-8 "*6We have gifts that differ according to the grace given to us: prophecy, in proportion to faith; 7<u>ministry, in ministering</u>; the teacher, in teaching; 8the encourager, in encouragement; the giver, in sincerity; the leader, in diligence; the compassionate, in cheerfulness.*" I underline ministering in Romans 12:7, because ministry is not a call to change jobs; it's simply a call to use our gifts, talents, virtues, and expertise in some way to help others (e.g., helping someone move their furniture, volunteering in church (e.g., singing in church, teaching the Word of God), or simply performing a random act of kindness.)

People are capable of performing random acts of kindness and people are even capable of performing heroic acts, but becoming a self-for-others is an ongoing call to seek the glory of God in some way that helps others. St. Irenaeus [130-201] told us that "The glory of God is man [humanity.]" In other words, we were created to be the glory of God, and becoming a self-for-others is one way to become the glory of God and return to our original destiny to live eternally incorruptible in the glory of God. St. Paul assures us in 2 Corinthians 3:18 "¹⁸And all of us, with unveiled faces, seeing the glory of the Lord as though reflected in a mirror, <u>are being transformed into the same image from one degree of glory to another</u>; for this comes from the Lord, the Spirit." For Catholic believers, we hope that our lives lead us to the kingdom of God, but we know that our salvation isn't guaranteed; it remains a gift from God. Becoming a self-for-others helps us to complete our transformation into the glory of God and return to our original design, in Genesis 1:26 and Wisdom 2:23.

Responding to God's Presence and Love through Our Joy and Thanksgiving

In my opinion, we continue to develop our relationship with God by expressing our joy and thanksgiving for all of God's gifts and blessings in our lives. The source of our joy comes from a deeper, positive, loving, personal relationship with God (e.g., Psalm 100:1-5.) The scriptures give us many examples of rejoicing in God. Nehemiah led some of the Israelites back from captivity and thanks to King Cyrus of Persia the Israelites completed rebuilding the walls and the gates of Jerusalem. The Israelites celebrated this occasion with prayer and joy in Nehemiah 8:10 "¹⁰Then he [Ezra] said to them, 'Go your way, eat the fat and drink sweet wine and send portions of them to those for whom nothing is prepared, for this day is holy to our LORD; and do not be grieved, for the joy of the LORD is your strength.'" The psalmist understood that God was the way to complete our joy, in Psalm 16:11 "¹¹You show me the path of life. In your presence there is fullness of joy; in your right hand are pleasures forevermore." Similarly, St. Paul wrote his letter to the Philippians from a prison cell, and he talked about his joy in the Lord throughout his letter (e.g., Philippians 4:4 "⁴Rejoice in the Lord always; again I will say, Rejoice.")

God gives us the gift of joy to complete our own happiness, in John 15:11 "¹¹I have said these things to you so that <u>my joy may be in you</u>, and that your joy may be complete." We are joyful because we live in the safety, security, and peace of God, through Jesus' Spirit that dwells in us. For Judeo-Christian believers, we're assured of our joy because we believe that we're never alone, in Hebrews 13:5 "I will never leave you or forsake you." God is the basis for our joy, and we should never stop thanking God for our gifts and blessings. The scriptures give us many examples of rejoicing in

God (e.g., Psalm 37:4 tells us to delight in the Lord and He will satisfy the joys of our hearts); St. Paul tells us that joy is one of the fruits of the Spirit indwelling in us in Galatians 5:22; and Luke's Gospel describes the joy of Jesus' seventy evangelists, who He sent out to tell everyone about the coming kingdom [reign] of God in Luke 10:17 "[17]<u>The seventy returned with joy</u>, saying, 'Lord, in your name even the demons submit to us!'"

In the Catechism of the Catholic Church, we learn that "God does not abandon his creatures to themselves. He not only gives them being and existence, but also, and at every moment, upholds and sustains them in being, enables them to act and brings them to their final end. Recognizing this utter dependence with respect to the Creator is a source of wisdom and freedom, of joy and confidence."[74]

We need to constantly thank God, because His steadfast love endures forever, in Psalm 103:8 "[8]The LORD is merciful and gracious, slow to anger and abounding in steadfast love." We must never let anyone or anything steal our joy. Instead, we need to constantly thank God for all the gifts and blessings in our lives (e.g., in our hope of eternal life with God in John 17:3.) Our joy is just one of many reasons for thanking God, who is the source of our strength. We need to continually thank God for all His gifts and blessings (e.g., Psalm 91:1-2

---

[74] "Catechism of the Catholic Church," article 301

"¹You who live in the shelter of the Most High, who abide in the shadow of the Almighty, ²will say to the Lord, 'My refuge and my fortress; my God, in whom I trust.'") We're thankful for God's unending gifts to us including God's creation, mercy, forgiveness, security, peace, and our salvation. We thank Jesus for His indwelling Holy Spirit, who guides us and helps us through the Word of God, and for God's many promises to us (e.g., the gift of resurrection into eternal life with God in John 14:1-3.) Catholic believers thank God and praise God in Mass by reciting prayers and singing hymns to the glory and majesty of God. In thanking God, we acknowledge that God is the source of our lives, our gifts, and our hopes in God's promises.

Part Five:

Responding to God's Presence and Love in Community

CHAPTER TEN

We Need to Respond to God's Presence and Love in Community

In part five of my book, I describe our need to respond to God's presence and love by worshipping God in a religious community, because the most obvious place to find God's presence and love is in His metaphorical home, the church, the synagogue, etc. The word "church" means a convocation or an assembly, and every church is grounded in the community it serves. In Florent Gaboriau's wonderful book *The Conversion of Edith Stein*, he quotes St. Augustine's commentary on John: "There must be special places on earth for the solemn praise of God, places where this praise is formed into the greatest perfection of which humankind is capable. From such places it can ascend to heaven for the whole church and have an influence on the church's members; it can awaken the interior life in them and make them zealous for external unanimity."[75]

---

[75] Florent Gaboriau, *The Conversion of Edith Stein*, 85 [St. Augustine, Commentary on John, tract 7]

We need to respond to God in community because we live our lives in community, and because God's love is always present, in Matthew 18:20, when two or more are gathered in His name. Religious communities provide us with an opportunity for fellowship with likeminded believers. And community worship gives us a special way to find God's presence and love (e.g., through the communities' beautiful music, liturgies, and traditions.)

There are many different religious communities that worship the one true God in their own unique ways; so, I gratefully acknowledge the wonderful contributions of my Jewish and Protestant brothers and sisters in their respective churches and synagogues and I acknowledge other communities of faith that are dedicated to obeying and serving the one true God. In addition, based on Acts 10:34-35, I acknowledge and pray for all individuals who are unable to participate in a religious community (e.g., for political reasons), but still manage to do what is acceptable to God.

Religious communities provide their believers with a gateway to God's promises (e.g., God's steadfast love, mercy, and abundant life) and an opportunity to support the various ministries of those religious communities (e.g., providing food and clothing to the needy, teaching and learning the Word of God, and providing community celebrations.) In addition, churches and synagogues provide further resources to help answer our prayers and questions.

Final thoughts

I want to thank everyone who took the time to read my book, and I sincerely hope that it helped someone to find God's presence and love [God's amazing grace] in their life and in the process that it helped them to answer some of their never-ending questions (e.g., why am I here?) It remains my belief that only God can fill the holes that we find in our daily lives, because we're designed and created to search for and respond to God's presence and love.

Bibliography

Allen, Leslie C., *Jeremiah – The Old Testament Library Series*, Louisville: Westminster John Knox Press, 2008

Arnal, William E., *Jesus and the Village Scribes*, Minneapolis, MN: Fortress Press, 2001

Banks, Robert J., *Paul's Idea of Community – Revised edition*, Peabody Massachusetts, Hendrickson Publishers, Inc., 1994

Blenkinsopp, J., *A History of Prophecy in Israel – 2nd Edition*, Louisville: Westminster John Knox Press, 1998

Bonhoeffer, Dietrich, *The Cost of Discipleship*, New York, London, Toronto, Sydney, Tokyo, Singapore: A Touchstone Book, Simon & Schuster, 1959

Bovon, Francois, Matthews, Christopher R., *The Acts of Philip, A New Translation*, Baylor University Press, Waco Texas, 2012

Bright, John, *The Kingdom of God*, Nashville Tennessee: Abingdon-Cokesbury Press, 1952

Bright, John, *A History of Israel, Fourth Edition*, Philadelphia, Pennsylvania: Westminster John Knox Press, 2000

Bright, John, *The Authority of the Old Testament*, Nashville Tennessee: Abingdon-Cokesbury Press, 1967

Brown, Raymond SS, *The Gospel and Epistles of John*, Collegeville Minnesota: Liturgical Press, 1988

Brown, Raymond SS, *An Introduction to NT Christology*, New York/Mahwah: Paulist Press, 1994

Browning, W.R.F., *A Dictionary of the Bible*, Oxford, New York: Oxford University Press, 1996

Buber, Martin, *I and Thou*, A Touchstone Book, Tr. By Walter Kaufmann, New York, NY, Simon & Schuster, 1970

Burrows, Ruth, *Fire Upon the Earth*, Denville, New Jersey: Dimension Books, 1981

Byrne, Brendan SJ, *Romans*, Sacra Pagina Series, Collegeville Minnesota: Liturgical Press, 1996

Childs, Brevard S., *Introduction to the Old Testament as Scripture*, Philadelphia: Fortress Press, 1979

Childs, Brevard S., *Isaiah*, The Old Testament Library Series, Louisville: Westminster John Knox Press, 2001

Chadwick, Henry, *The Early Church*, Revised Edition, London England: Penguin Group, 1993

Clifford, Richard J. SJ, *Wisdom*, New Collegeville Biblical Commentary, Collegeville Minnesota: Liturgical Press, 2012

Clifford, Richard J. SJ, *The Wisdom Literature*, Nashville TE: Abingdon Press, 1998

Clifford, Richard J. SJ, *Psalms 1–72*, Nashville TE: Abingdon Press, 2002

Clifford, Richard J. SJ, *Psalms 73–150*, Nashville TE: Abingdon Press, 2003

Clifford, Richard J. SJ, *Deuteronomy*, Wilmington, Delaware: Michael Glazier, Inc., 1989

Clifford, Richard J. SJ, *Fair Spoken and Persuauding: An interpretation of Second Isaiah*, New York, NY: Paulist Press, 1984

Collins, John J., *The Apocalyptic Imagination*, 2nd Edition, Grand Rapids, Michigan/ Cambridge, UK: William B. Eerdmans Publishing Company, 1998

Coogan, Michael D., Ed., *The Oxford History of the Biblical World*, New York, NY: Oxford University Press, Inc., 1998

Cook, Stephen L., *Prophecy & Apocalypticism: The Postexilic Social Setting*, Minneapolis, MN: Fortress Press, 1995

Darwin, Charles, *The Origin o Species*, London, England: Signet Classics, an imprint of New American Library, a Division of Penguin Group [USA], 1958

Dunn, James, *Christology in the Making – 2nd Edition*, Grand Rapids, Michigan/Cambridge, UK: William B. Eerdmans Publishing Company, 1996

Dych, William V. SJ, *Karl Rahner*, Wilmington, Delaware: Michael Glazier, Inc., 1992

Egan, Harvey D. SJ, *Karl Rahner–Mystic of Everyday Life*, New York, NY: The Crossroad Publishing Co., 1998

Eichrodt, Walter, *Ezekiel*, The Old Testament Library Series, Philadelphia: Westminster Press, Translation @ SCM Press Ltd, 1970

Fitzmyer, Joseph A. SJ, *The Gospel According to Luke*, X-XXIV, The Anchor Bible, Volume 28A, Garden City, NY: Doubleday & Company Inc., 1985

Fitzmyer, Joseph A. SJ, *The Acts of the Apostles*, A New Translation, Introduction, and Commentary, The Anchor Yale Bible, New Haven and London: Yale University Press, 1998

Fitzmyer, Joseph A. SJ, *Paul and His Theology – 2nd Edition*, Englewood Cliffs, NJ: Prentice Hall, Inc., a Simon Schuster Company, 1989

Fuller, Reginald, *The Foundations of NT Christology*, New York: Charles Scribner's Sons, 1965

Gaarder, Jostein, *Sophie's World*, Farrar, Straus, & Giroux, Tr. Paulette Moller, Berkley edition, New York, NY: The Berkley Publishing Group, 1996

Gaboriau, Florent, *The Conversion of Edith Stein*, Tr. Ralph McInerny, South Bend, Indiana: St. Augustine's Press, 2018

Gonzalez, Justo L., *The Story of Christianity, Volumes I & II*, New York, NY: Harper San Francisco, A division of Harper-Collins Publishers, 1984, 1985

Gonzalez, Justo L., *A History of Christian Thought*, Nashville, TE: Abingdon Press, 1970

Gowan, D. E., *Theology of the Prophetic Books: The Death and Resurrection of Israel*, Louisville: Westminster John Knox Press, 1998

Groome, Thomas H., *Christian Religious Education*, New York, NY: Harper San Francisco, A division of Harper-Collins publishers, 1980

Groome, Thomas H., *Sharing Faith*, New York, NY: Harper San Francisco, A division of Harper-Collins publishers, 1991

Haight, Roger SJ, *The Experience and Language of Grace*, New York/Ramsey/Toronto: Paulist Press, 1979

Haight, Roger SJ, *Dynamics of Theology*, Mahwah, NJ: Paulist Press, 1990

Haight, Roger SJ, *Jesus Symbol of God*, Maryknoll, New York: Orbis Books, 1999

Harrington, Daniel J. SJ, *Interpreting the New Testament*, Collegeville, Minnesota: A Michael Glazier Book, Liturgical Press, 1979

Harrington, Daniel J. SJ, *The Maccabean Revolt*, Wilmington, Delaware: Michael Glazier, Inc., 1988

Harrington, Daniel J. SJ, *The Gospel of Matthew*, Sacra Pagina Series, Collegeville Minnesota: Liturgical Press, 1991

Harrington, Daniel J. SJ, *Paul on the Mystery of Israel*, Collegeville Minnesota: Liturgical Press, 1992

Harrington, Daniel J. SJ, <u>Who is Jesus – Why is He Important?</u>, Franklin, Wisconsin: Sheed & Ward, 1999

Hayes, Zachary, OFM, *Visions of a Future*, Collegeville, Minnesota: A Michael Glazier Book, The Liturgical Press, 1991

Hentz, Otto SJ, *The Hope of the Christian*, Collegeville, Minnesota: A Michael Glazier Book, The Liturgical Press, 1997

Holmen, T., "The Alternatives of the Kingdom," Zeitschrift fur die neutestamentliche Disenchant 87-88 (1996-97) 204-229

Hooker, Morna D., *The Gospel According to Saint Mark*, Black's New Testament Commentaries, London: Hendrickson Publishers, Inc., 3rd Printing, 1999

Huebsch, Bill, *A New Look at Grace-8th Printing*, Mystic, CT: Twenty Third Publications, 1999

Johnson, Luke Timothy, *The Gospel of Luke*, Sacra Pagina Series, Collegeville Minnesota: Liturgical Press, 1991

Jozo, Zovko, Fr., *A Man Named Father Jozo*, Milford OH: The Richle Foundation, 1989

Kant, Immanuel, *Fundamental Principles of the Metaphysic Morals*, Tr. T. K. Abbott, Buffalo, NY: Prometeus Books, 1988

Kavanaugh, Kieran, O.C.D., Rodriquez, Otilio, O.C.D., *The Collected Works of Teresa of Avila*, Washington DC: ICS Publications, 1980

Kavanaugh, Kieran, O.C.D., Rodriquez, Otilio, O.C.D., *The Collected Works of St. John of the Cross*, Washington DC: ICS Publications, 1991

Keenan, James F. SJ, *Virtues for Ordinary Christians*, Franklin, Wisconsin: Sheed & Ward, 1999

Kloppenborg, John S., *Excavating Q*, Minneapolis, MN: Fortress Press, 2000

Lake, Kirsopp, *The Apostolic Fathers, volumes I & II*, Loeb Classical Library, Ed. by G. P. Goold, Cambridge MA, Harvard University Press, First Published in 1912, reprinted 1914–1998

Lynch, William F. SJ, *Images of Hope*, London: University of Notre Dame Press, 3rd printing, 1987

Lyke, Larry L., *I Will Espouse You Forever*, Nashville TE: Abingdon Press, 2007

Mack, Burton L., *The Lost Gospel: The Book of Q*, New York, NY, Harper San Francisco, A division of Harper-Collins Publishers, 1993

MacMullen, Ransay, *Christianizing the Roman Empire A.D.100-400*, New Haven and London: Yale University Press, 1984

Martini, Cardinal Carlo Maria, *The Gospel According to St. Paul*, originally published Milan, Italy, Ancora Editrice, English Translation, Ljamville, MD: The Word Among Us Press, 2008

Matera, Frank J., *New Testament Christologies*, Louisville, Kentucky: Westminster John Knox Press, 1999

McDermott, Brian O. SJ, *Word Become Flesh: Dimensions of Christology*, Collegeville, Minnesota: A Michael Glazier Book, The Liturgical Press, 1993

Meeks, Wayne A., *The First Urban Christians*, 2nd Edition, New Haven and London: Yale University Press, 2003

Meier, John P., *A Marginal Jew, Rethinking the Historical Jesus*, Volume One – The Roots of the Problem and the Person, New York, London, Toronto: Doubleday, 1991

Meier, John P., *A Marginal Jew, Rethinking the Historical Jesus*, Volume Two – Mentor, Message, and Miracles, New York, London, Toronto: Doubleday, 1994

Meier, John P., *A Marginal Jew, Rethinking the Historical Jesus*, Volume Three – Companions and Competitors, New York, London, Toronto: Doubleday, 2001

Meissner, W.W. SJ, *Thy Kingdom Come*, Kansas City, MO: Sheed & Ward, 1995

Merton, Thomas, *Contemplative Prayer*, New York, NY: Image Books, Doubleday, 1971

Merton, Thomas, *New Seeds of Contemplation*, New York, NY: The Abbey of Gethsemani, Inc., 1968

Merton, Thomas, *Zen and the Birds of Appetite*, New York, NY: The Abbey of Gethsemani, Inc., 1961

Metz, Johannes Baptist, *Poverty of Spirit*, Tr. John Drury, [Inclusive Language Version by Carole Farris], New York/Mahwah, NJ: Paulist Press, 1998

Metz, Johannes Baptist, *A Passion for God*, Tr. J. Matthew Ashley, New York/Mahwah, NJ: Paulist Press, 1998

Metzger, Bruce M., Murphy, Roland E., *The New Oxford Annotated Bible, The New Revised Standard Version, w/Apocrypha*, Oxford, New York, Toronto: Oxford University Press, 1994

Meyer, Stephen C., *Signature in a Cell*, New York, NY, Harper One [A division of Harper-Collins Publishers], 2009

Meyer, Stephen C., *Darwin's Doubt*, New York, NY, Harper One [A division of Harper-Collins Publishers], 2013

Meyer, Stephen C., *Return of the God Hypothesis*, New York, NY, Harper One [A division of Harper-Collins Publishers], 2021

Michaels, J. R., "Almsgiving and the Kingdom Within: Tertullian on Luke 17:21," Catholic Biblical Quarterly 60 (1998) 475-483.

Milton, John, *Paradise Lost*, London England: Penguin Classics, Edited with an Introduction by John Leonard, 2000

Modras, Ronald E., *Ignatian Humanism*, Chicago, IL: Loyola Press, 2000

Moloney, Francis J., S.D.B., *The Gospel of John*, Sacra Pagina Series, Collegeville Minnesota: Liturgical Press, 1991

Moltmann, Jurgen, *The Trinity and the Kingdom*, Minneapolis, MN: Fortress Press, 1993

Mott, Michael, *The Seven Mountains of Thomas Merton*, New York: Harcourt Brace & Company, 1993

Murphy, Roland E. O. Carm., *The Tree of Life, 2nd edition*, Grand Rapids, MI: William B. Erdman Publishing Company, 1990

Nietzsche, Friedrich, *Beyond Good and Evil*, Tr. Helen Zimmern, Lexington, KY: 2018,

originally published in Leipzig, Germany by **C. G. Naumann publishers**, 1886

O'Brien, David J., Shannon, Thomas A., *Catholic Social Thought: The Documentary Heritage, 2nd Printing*, Maryknoll, New York: Orbis Books, 1995

O'Collins, Gerald SJ, *Christology: A Biblical, Historical, and Systematic Study of Jesus*, New York, New York: Oxford University Press, 1995

O'Donnell, John J. SJ, *The Mystery of the Triune God*, New York, NY: Paulist Press, 1989

O'Donnell, John J. SJ, *Hans Urs von Balthasar*, Collegeville, Minnesota: A Michael Glazier Book, Liturgical Press, 1992

O'Donovan, Leo J., *A World of Grace*, New York: The Seabury Press, Inc. 1980

O'Meara, Thomas F., *God in the World*, Collegeville, Minnesota: A Michael Glazier Book, Liturgical Press, 2007

Rahner, Karl SJ, *Foundations of Christian Faith*, Tr. By William V. Dych SJ, New York, NY: The Crossroad Publishing Company, 1995

Rahner, Karl SJ, *Hearer of the Word*, Tr. By Joseph Donceel, [Ed. with Introduction by Andrew Tallon], New York, NY: The Continuum Publishing Company, 1994

Rahner, Karl SJ, *Spirit in the World*, Tr. By William Dych SJ, New York, NY: Herder and Herder 1968

Rahner, Karl SJ, "On the Theology of Worship," Theological Investigations XIX ,(New York: Crossroad, 1983), 141-149

Rahner, Karl SJ, "Nature and Grace," <u>Theological Investigations IV</u>, (London: Baltimore Helicon press, 1996) 165-187

Rahner, Karl SJ, "The One Christ and the Universality of Salvation," <u>Theological Investigations XVI</u> (New York: Crossroad, 1979) 199-224

Ratzinger, Joseph Cardinal, <u>Catechism of the Catholic Church</u>, Interdicasterial Working Group of the Holy See, Liberia Editrice Vatican [**Vatican Publishing** House], Citta del Vaticano [Vatican City], 1994

Reumann, John, *Righteousness in the New Testament*, Responses by Joseph A. Fitzmyer SJ and Jerome D. Quinn, Ramsey NJ: Paulist Press, 1982

Rousseau, Jean-Jacques, *The Social Contract*, New York, New York: Classic Books International, First Printing, 2010

Sachs, John R. SJ, *The Christian Vision of Humanity*, Collegeville, Minnesota: A Michael Glazier Book, Liturgical Press, 1991

Sachs, John R. SJ, "Do Not Stifle the Spirit: Karl Rahner, the Legacy of Vatican II, and its Urgency for Theology Today," *The Catholic Theological Society of America, Proceedings of the Fifty-first Annual Convention Volume 51*: (New York: St John's University, 1996), 15-44

Schroeder, Rev. H. J. OP, Translated and Introduced, *The Canons and Decrees of the Council of Trent*, Rockford, Illinois: Tan Books and Publishers, Inc., 1978

Sobrino, Jon SJ, *Jesus the Liberator*, Maryknoll, New York: Orbis Books, 1998

St. Anselm, *Proslogian*, Translated and Introduced by M. J. Charlesworth, London: University of Notre Dame Press, 1979 [First edition published by Oxford University Press in 1965]

St. Aquinas, Thomas, *Introduction to St. Thomas Aquinas, the Summa Theologica, The Summa Contra Gentiles*, Edited by Anton C. Pegis, NY, NY: McGraw-Hill, Inc. 1948

St. Augustine, *Confessions*, London, England: Penguin Books, Clays Ltd, St. Ives plc, 1961

St. Teresa of Avila, *The Interior Castle*, London: Fount Paperbacks, 1995

Stegman, Thomas D. SJ, *Opening the Door of Faith*, Mahwah, NJ: Paulist Press, 2015

Sweetland, Dennis M., *Our Journey with Jesus: Discipleship According to Luke-Acts*, A Collegeville, Minnesota: Michael Glazier Book, Liturgical Press, 1990

Tate, W. Randolph, *Biblical Interpretation, third edition*, Hendrickson Publishers, Inc. Peabody MA, 2008

Vatican Council II, Volume 1, *The Conciliar and post Council Documents, New Revised Edition*, General Editor: Austin Flannery OP, Northport NY: Costello Publishing Company, Inc., 1998

Viviano, Benedict T., *The Kingdom of God in History*, Collegeville Minnesota: Liturgical Press, 1991

Von Balthasar, Hans Urs SJ, *Prayer*, Tr. Graham Harrison, San Francisco, CA: Ignatius Press, 1986

Vorgrimler, Herbert, *Understanding Karl Rahner*, New York, NY: The Crossroad Publishing Company, 1986

Weiser, Arthur, *The Psalms*, The Old Testament Library Series, Philadelphia: The Westminster Press, 1962

Wright, N. T., *Jesus and the Victory of God, Christian Origins, and the Questions of God – Volume Two*, Minneapolis: Fortress Press, 1996

Wright, N. T., *Paul*, Minneapolis: Fortress Press, 2005